"An excellent introduction to the people and issues of Amazonia, written by somebody with worldwide knowledge of development pitfalls.**"**
— **Robin Hanbury-Tenison**
President, Survival International

"… illuminates urgent human and environmental issues… reaches the roots of why our work to save the world's rainforests is so important.**"**
— **The Rainforest Foundation**

"… orchestrates a medley of voices as diverse, combative, frustrating, and exciting as the Amazon itself.**"**
— **Michael H. Robinson, Tropical Biologist**
Zoological Park Director, Washington, D.C.

VOICES
FROM THE
AMAZON

VOICES
FROM THE
AMAZON

Binka Le Breton

KUMARIAN PRESS

Kumarian Press Books for a World that Works

Dedication

To Juliet, best of traveling companions
and Robin, best of all

Voices from the Amazon.
Published 1993 by Kumarian Press, Inc. 630 Oakwood Avenue, Suite 119,
West Hartford, Connecticut 06110-1529 USA

Cover design by Marc Bellefleur

Book production supervised by Jenna Dixon
Copyedited by Linda Lotz
Text design and typeset by Jenna Dixon
Proofread by Jolene Robinson
Map by Marie Litterer
Index prepared by Barbara DeGennaro

Printed in the United States of America on recycled acid-free paper
by Edwards Brothers. Text printed with soy-based ink.

Library of Congress Cataloging-in-Publication Data
Le Breton, Binka.
    Voices from the Amazon / Binka Le Breton.
        p.   cm. — (Kumarian Press books for a world that works)
      Includes bibliographical references and index.
      ISBN 1-56549-021-5 (pbk. : alk. paper)
      1. Man—Influence on nature—Amazon River Region. 2. Environmen-
tal degradation—Amazon River Region. 3. Rural development—Environmental aspects—Amazon River Region. 4. Forest products industry—
Amazon River Region—Environmental aspects. 5. Amazon River
Region—Social conditions. 6. Amazon River Region—Economic conditions. I. Title. II. Series.
GF532.A4L43   1993
333.75'0981'1—dc20   93-16349

97 96 95 94 93   5 4 3 2 1   First printing, 1993

CONTENTS

Frontispiece: Map of Brazil   *ii*
Foreword by Thomas E. Lovejoy   *vii*
Preface   *ix*
Reader's Reference   *xiii*

1   Amazônia   1
2   Inside Rondônia   5
3   Indians   9
4   Loggers   21
5   River People   34
6   Miners   45
7   Settlers   58
8   Ranchers   76
9   Rubber Tappers   88
10 Idealists   104
11 A Chorus of Comments   117
12 What Next?   130

Epilogue   *139*
Bibliography   *145*
Index   *147*

FOREWORD

My first arrival in the Amazon was late at night. The Pan American flight had followed a route laid down for the Allied war effort: island hopping down the Caribbean followed by the tin-roofed airport at Georgetown, Guyana, then Paramaribo, Suriname, and finally Belém. The heat and humidity were palpable as we edged our way through the formalities in the terminal open to the night air and its vibrant sounds. By noon the following day, I was looking out at the muddy waters of the Bay of Guajara from the restaurant in the original fortifications of this seventeenth-century city grown to prominence during the rubber boom.

The slow rattle of fishing boat diesels and silent swooping vultures cast a spell of utter timelessness. It was 1965, still during what one Brazilian military figure nostalgically termed the romantic era of the Amazon. There was a strong sense of isolation, almost as if the Amazon enfolded itself about you and snuffed out any sense of connection to the rest of the world. Only two million people were then living in the Amazon of Brazil. And for me as an aspiring graduate student, it was a naturalist's paradise where discovery was the rule of every day.

There was little indication of the pace and scale of change to come. The Transamazon Highway scheme had yet to be conceived. The Manaus economic free zone had yet to bring a second boom to the rubber capital moldering since early in the century. The side-scanning radar project, RADAM, had yet to identify promising areas for mineral extraction and the accidental discovery of the fabulous Carajas iron lode had yet to take place. Nor had the hordes of colonists poured into Rondônia and elsewhere, nor had the million gold miners fanned out across the basin polluting promiscuously with mercury and creating some of the most arresting scenes ever of seething lust for gold at Serra Pellada. This was before the moon landing and the space shuttle which later was to record a smoke cloud the size of Texas over Amazônia. Indeed as I write, it is hard, even for me, to grasp how much has changed in the ensuing twenty-eight years.

Today it is commonplace to hear concern expressed about the fate of the rain forest, of the Amazon and of its remaining indigenous peoples. It occurs in New York City living rooms, in Rio de Janeiro shops, and a multitude of other places. That is good and it is important. But today there are 17 million people in the Brazilian Amazon and until their situations and aspiration are dealt with thoughtfully and carefully, the larger problems of deforestation, loss of biological diversity, and indigenous peoples simply cannot be resolved.

This volume provides the opportunity to hear the voices of the different inhabitants of the Amazon. Often there is error in their understanding of particular aspects of the quandary. Yet there is a reality to their perception which must must be heard and understood for what it really means or it will stand in the way of truly addressing the problems. The diversity of voices delineated so clearly in this volume is something to which few have access.

The drama of the Amazon today is not just environmental. It is also very human. Binka Le Breton's acute ear helps us better understand that drama, and reminds us how important it is just to listen.

Thomas E. Lovejoy
Assistant Secretary for External Affairs
Smithsonian Institution

PREFACE

It all started with the milkman.

I was visiting my mother in England and enjoying breakfast in her sunny kitchen when the milkman stuck his head in through the window.

"Living in Brazil now, are you?" he asked, banging the bottles down on the windowsill. "Well, I hope you'll stop them cutting down the Amazon. It's a real shame what they're doing to the forest and all those Indians."

Unwittingly, he had struck at the heart of one of my deepest concerns. Since moving to Brazil in 1989, I had watched with increasing unease as the small farmers who were our neighbors attempted to stave off starvation for a few months producing illicit charcoal by hacking away at the tiny remains of the Atlantic rain forest. This forest once stretched over an area of 3,600 square miles, from Rio Grande do Norte as far as Rio Grande do Sul, near the Uruguayan frontier. Today it is reduced to three percent of its former extent.

Further north lies the huge rain forest that covers most of the 2.2 million square miles of the Amazon basin. In Brazilian Amazônia, an area of 1.35 million square miles that comprises 57 percent of the entire territory of Brazil, the forest is being mercilessly beaten back as people flock into the region to seek their fortunes. Development seems to be synonymous with destruction, yet most Amazonians remain obstinately poor.

Let me come clean at once. I am a concert pianist, not a development expert, except perhaps by marriage. My husband, Robin, has worked as an agricultural economist in Africa, Asia, and Latin America for twenty years—mostly for the World Bank, but also for the Commonwealth Development Corporation (United Kingdom) and the Food and Agriculture Organization of the United Nations.

I have lived all over the developing world, and my family has always been mixed up in the business of trying to help people make a better life for themselves. Our most recent overseas assignment had been in the dry and desperate northeast of Brazil. Three years of battling the bureaucracy of the Brazilian government had just about finished my husband. He had spent his spare moments dreaming of how to make the desert blossom and had fired himself up with the idea of buying a piece of land and transforming it. "I've been preaching sustainable development for years," he pointed out. "Now it's time to put it into practice."

We'd been through a "Let's buy a palace in Rajasthan" period; we'd done a "How about a ranch in New Mexico?" bit; and now Robin was suggesting that we try our luck in some of the harshest, most miserable land in the world.

I was immediately assailed by every doubt and fear in the book, and I gave Robin the benefit of each one in exhaustive detail. To me they seemed eminently reasonable. To Robin they seemed a combination of cowardice and procrastination.

In the end I ran out of excuses, so we compromised and moved to an abandoned *fazenda* in the mountains further south.

It had once been a prosperous coffee region, but the price of coffee had declined steadily over the years. Small farmers who had formerly owned Volkswagen Beetles and five-kilowatt generators were now back to pony carts and kerosene lamps. They just couldn't make a go of it; that's why they were cutting the forest.

I took the milkman's challenge personally, as did my daughter Juliet. Newly graduated from college, she had already announced her intention to spend a year in Brazil and take a closer look at the Amazon. Our family had visited the Amazon before. We'd squashed ourselves into the little boats that travel between Belém and Benjamin Constant on the borders of Peru and Colombia, we'd canoed to some of the small villages and stayed with the Indians and the river people, and we'd spent hours in buses stuck on muddy Amazon roads. We had already devoured every book we could find on the Amazon, and the more we learned, the more fascinated we became. But apart from coffee table books on the vanishing Indians, we couldn't find anything substantial about the two million people who live deep in the Brazilian rain forest. And since they are the ones who are largely responsible for cutting it down, we decided to go meet them and find out what they had to say.

Many different types of people are contributing to the loss of the rain forest. Deforestation starts with roads: roads put in by loggers to extract timber, roads put in by ranchers to give them access to their lands, and roads put in by the government to open up the interior. Roads bring people, and people bring fire and chain saws. The government installs development schemes and hydro projects; settlements spring up, and settlers fan out into the forest. Last to come are the land grabbers, who pounce on abandoned plots. Each one contributes to deforestation, and as fragile forestlands cease to support settlers, they are forced to move on, and the cycle continues.

Juliet and I talked it over. We pored over maps. We discovered, to our alarm, that our target area was roughly the size of India. We would have to narrow it down.

"How about going to Rondônia?" said Juliet, pointing to a small state tucked away in the far west, bordering Bolivia. "That's where the government put in the colonization schemes. Knocked down the forest and brought in thousands of people to settle the state. There's a big development project called Polonoroeste up there. I studied it in an anthropology course last year. And look, Rondônia's right next to Acre."

I found the state of Acre tucked under the armpit of Peru, its western boundary less than 500 miles from the Pacific Ocean.

"Acre used to be the big rubber state," continued Juliet. "Remember the murder of Chico Mendes and all the fuss about the rubber tappers? I'd like to know if anything has changed for them, now that things have quieted down. I think we should contrast the two states. Take a look at the gold mining on the Madeira River. Get out to the Indian reserves if we can and talk to the settlers and the ranchers. There are cocaine smugglers and arms dealers and heaven knows what else up there. Real Wild West stuff. Maybe we could write something."

Having selected the geographical location, we then set out to find suitable candidates to interview. Here we were assisted by a variety of church, state, and private organizations. Once on site, we encountered little difficulty in obtaining interviews. Brazilians are friendly and open, and everyone—with the single exception of Sidney the rancher—spoke freely. Even Sidney mellowed during the course of the conversation. All the interviews were conducted in Portuguese, except those with English speakers: Nick Burch the forester and Ludwig the gold miner. Charlie the gypsy spoke a mixture of Spanish and Portuguese. Interviews were taped or written, in accordance with the preference of the speaker; most were unaccustomed to tape recorders and preferred to speak without them. I translated and edited these conversations where necessary.

Our thanks are due to all those who shared their experiences and frequently their hospitality with us. Also, thanks to the following: Joannie, Sam, and Jenny in England; Sara, James, and Luiza in Brazil; and Marston, Sharon, Alice, Jim, and Jeannie in the States. Special thanks to my husband Robin for his unstinting support and affection. I treasure his comment on his pianist-turned-writer wife: "It's a lot quieter being married to a writer."

READER'S REFERENCE

Glossary

ayahuasca	hallucinogenic drug
boto	Amazon dolphin
caboclos	forest people of mixed blood
cacique	Indian chief
candiru	Amazon fish
capoeira	invasive scrub; also degraded land covered with such scrub
chicha	corn beer
chimarrão	gourd for drinking *mate*
cupuaçu	Amazon fruit used in candy, desserts, and juice
deputado	state or federal representative
draga	dredger for gold mining
empate	peaceful protest against forest cutting
epadu	shade-grown cocaine
farinha	manioc flour
fazenda	large farm/ranch
fofoca	collection of dredgers (slang usage)
garimpeiro	gold miner
garimpo	gold mining area
genipapo	fruit used for dye
guaraná	fruit; a popular health drink made from guaraná fruit; also used in a soft drink
maloca	Indian house

marreteiro	trader
mate	kind of tea
pajé	medicine man
pium	sand fly
pistoleiro	gunman
poronga	lamp used by rubber tappers
ribeirinho	river person
seringal	rubber tapping area
seringueiro	rubber tapper
sertão	dry lands in the northeast
várzea	floodplain

Acronyms

CAPEMI	military pension fund
CERON	Rondonia Electric Company
FUNAI	Federal Indian Authority
FUNTAC	Acre government environmental research center
INCRA	Land Settlement Board
SUDAM	Amazon Development Authority
UDR	Democratic Rural Union
UNCED	United Nations Conference on Environment and Development
UNEP	United Nations Environmental Program
UNI	Union of Indigenous Nations
VARIG	Brazil's largest airline

1

AMAZÔNIA

A very populous and rich land, [from which] would be attained great treasures.
—Gonzalo Pizarro, 1541

The bus pulled out of the station in Brasília, the gleaming capital city designed by the Kubitschek administration (1956–61) to point to the Amazon. We passed the last shantytown and headed off across the high plateau, following the Brazilian dream to El Dorado.

Twenty-four hours later we pulled into the cavernous concrete bus station in Cuiabá, capital of the state of Mato Grosso. It was empty and echoing. The only signs of life were around the bus marked "Porto Velho," which is the capital of Rondônia.

It looked like the whole world was heading for Rondônia. Families were hovering around their piled-up possessions: boxes, bags, cooking pots, mattresses, and shapeless bundles sewn up in hessian sacks. Small children clutched bottles, blankets, and comforters. Their anxious mothers tried unsuccessfully to round them up, while their fathers squatted in little groups and smoked. Everyone wore their best jeans, with cowboy hats and studded leather belts for the men and tight fluorescent spandex tops for the women. Some of the men strutted about in shirts open to the navel, displaying heavy gold chains on hairy chests. They had found their El Dorado. The rest were still looking.

Somewhere a loudspeaker crackled an incomprehensible announcement. A very small boy struggled to load the unwieldy baggage into the underbelly of the bus. The driver, immaculate in palest pink, honked his horn. After a wild scramble for seats, we were off—to the promised land.

A few hours later we reached the bridge over the Paraguay River. It was heavily guarded by youthful soldiers in camouflage and painted faces. They searched the bus slowly and methodically, looking for drugs. They don't call this the TransCoca Highway for nothing.

Juliet and I gazed out the window at an endless flat landscape. The jungle seemed to be in disorderly retreat. The road knifed through mile after mile of cleared and burned land, occasionally passing small patches of cultivation. Sometimes we saw a small wooden shack, sometimes a few cattle. In the hazy distance the forest loomed, oddly menacing.

We had ample time to reflect on why we had come. The Amazon forest is burning, the Indians are dying, and paradise is being lost. Why do we care? Is it because our worst fears about global warming may be coming true? Do we understand that once the forest is gone, it is gone forever? Isn't extinction inevitable anyway? In a world of war and starvation, with dislocation and violence, in the face of recession and economic uncertainty, do we really have energy and compassion enough to care about the spotted owl? A few forest Indians? An undescribed and unknown species that may or may not be useful to us someday? Or do we, perhaps, perceive that there is still time to save something large and complex and immeasurably beautiful?

There is little margin for error. The genetic base of our food supply is dangerously small; in fact, seventy percent of what we eat comes from only eight major food crops. As we lose the wild ancestors of these species, our stocks of germ plasm will decrease dangerously—perhaps to the point where we are no longer able to breed the new cultivars we require.

We are losing priceless biological resources before we ever get the chance to find out what they are and how to use them. One in four major drugs already derives from a forest plant, and scientists tell us that there are at least 1,400 rain forest plant species with potential medicinal value. For all we know, the forest holds the answers to Alzheimer's, cancer, AIDS, or some new disease that hasn't even struck yet. We may never find those answers, because the forest won't be there anymore.

It's easy to worry about the extinction of cute and furry animals, but it's hard for most of us to get worked up over, say, nasty-looking insects. Yet somewhere in the forest there may be the one bug that could provide a crucial biological control for a predator ravaging our food crops. How long can that insect survive?

Juliet and I looked out the window at the fringes of the last great forest, irrevocably altered as the road goes through, bringing people and chain saws. We were entering the project area known as Polonoroeste, a development scheme designed and carried out with ample funding and expert technical advice. Done with the best of intentions, it nevertheless led to the destruction of the forest on a scale previously unimagined.

The government had looked west and had seen what appeared to be a huge, fertile, empty land. It decided to open up that land to provide homes for the homeless and food for the nation. But the government fell prey to one of the myths about Amazônia: the myth of the empty wilderness. It was 1.3 million square miles—the size of India—and they called it "a land without men for men without land." The government also saw in the Amazon the old dream of El Dorado—a place of inexhaustible riches. It set its sights not only on the land but also on the gold and minerals that lay beneath it.

Men and women from all over Brazil were lured by the gold in the rivers, minerals in the earth, land for the taking, and the nationalistic promise of "Greater Brazil." They came by the thousands. What they found was a land neither fertile nor empty. They found, to their surprise, Indians and river people and rubber tappers already living in the forest. And sometimes they found themselves in bloody conflict over the land.

The settlers learned that the soils were fragile, and that it was tough to clear the forest, tough to grow crops, and often impossible to market them. They found themselves poorly housed, poorly fed, poorly educated, and often in miserable health. They found themselves in a violent land without law, where contraband, drug trafficking, murder, and mayhem were the norms.

Their arrival was very nearly the end for the Indians. Within twenty years the indigenous population of Rondônia declined from 30,000 to 6,000. "We have been living in harmony with nature for thousands of years," said one of them. "Yet in less than 500 years outsiders have destroyed our forests, exterminated our wildlife, polluted our rivers and lakes, destroyed our cultural, religious, and ecological traditions, and enslaved and prostituted our people."

The settlers came to Rondônia in response to the government call. They stampeded up the BR-364, the Highway of Hope, and founded a new state. It brought death and destruction to the Indians, but to the settlers it brought lands and life.

2

INSIDE RONDÔNIA

A charnel house; a welter of putrefaction where men die like flies.

—PWC Co. of London, 1876

Juliet and I had traveled over 3,000 miles by bus—the trip took fifty-eight hours—and it was with considerable relief that we uncurled ourselves and stumbled out at a little town in the middle of Rondônia at four in the morning. We made our way to the small grubby hotel near the bus station, threw our packs on the floor, and squashed uncomfortably into the only available bed. It was a narrow, lumpy bed and the sheets smelled strongly of cigarette smoke, but we were grateful to be able to lie flat.

Our journey had taken us through miles of forestland that had been cleared and was now invaded by useless scrub. We had seen scores of small wooden houses, each with its hopeful little family and its burnt and ruined fields. We had stopped in the new towns that straggle along the road and heard the samba music relentlessly pounding out, night and day. We had felt the sticky heat, breathed in the choking dust, and rushed, like everyone else, for glasses of iced water. We were tired, hungry, stiff, and sleepy. We were beginning to feel like immigrants ourselves. But we were starting to build up a picture, however fragmentary, of life on the new frontier.

In 1960, the entire population of Rondônia numbered less than 100,000, all living along the rivers. By 1990, more than a million fortune seekers had streamed into Rondônia, and the sparsely populated jungle had become a brand new state.

What happened in the neighboring state of Acre was a little different. To start with, the area had been settled by rubber tappers from the northeast since the 1870s, the early days of the rubber boom. Wedged between Bolivia and Brazil, Acre had enjoyed brief glory as an independent republic, and its political struggles had bred a race of doughty fighters. Thirty years ago, when Rondônia was poised for its giant leap forward, Acre was still struggling along through the dying years of the rubber trade. Then the governor, inspired by the concept of Greater Brazil, decided to make his own bid for fame.

He wasn't interested in settlement schemes, although one or two sneaked in while his back was turned. His plan was to open up the state to ranching on a grand scale. This naturally led to the cutting and burning of large stretches of forest, and the government was as surprised as anyone when the forest people came out and started agitating for social justice. The rubber tappers began to form labor unions. With the murder of Chico Mendes in 1988, they acquired their own saint and martyr. Mendes had led his fellow rubber tappers into organized resistance against the big landowners who were trying to push them out. Although murder is common in the Amazon, this particular death focused international attention on Amazônia in general and Acre in particular. This was not at all the sort of fame the governor had been hoping for.

What sort of people came to the far west? They were, overwhelmingly, poor. They came in the hope of a better life. They pounded up the BR-364 in buses, trucks, pickups—anything that moved. They swarmed into the settlements, or into the forests if there was no land to be had elsewhere. They headed for the mining areas and dug for cassiterite (the chief source of tin) or dredged for gold. Some of them drifted to the towns and found what work they could. There they stayed, because they had no place else to go.

These days things are not going well in Rondônia. Many settlers have abandoned their plots, driven out by a combination of poor soils, poor transport, and lack of cash. Some of them are even beginning to leave, although it is hard to locate accurate figures. It is certainly easy to get a seat on the bus going in, but hard to get one on the bus going out.

Still, most Rondônians we talked to seemed to be happy with their state. It's a rickety-rackety place, but it's home. Most of them are proud of being pioneers, and there is one big difference between Rondônia and the south, where so many of the settlers came from: in Amazônia, there is still plenty of space for newcomers. There is a reasonable chance of making some sort of a life for oneself. On the downside, there is also a chance of getting shot. Here, power belongs to the man with the biggest gun, and the law of the jungle prevails.

The rich, though in the minority, usually have the biggest guns. Rich migrants came to Rondônia to get richer, and by and large they have succeeded. They set up businesses in logging, ranching, construction—any of the numerous enterprises that can be established when large areas of land are up for grabs. They came for the gold and the minerals. They came to buy up the settlers' abandoned plots and accumulate as much land as they could.

Things worked out very differently in Acre. For one thing, there was no road, which made getting to Acre excruciatingly difficult. By the end of 1991, the main road connection to the rest of the country had still not been completely paved, and within the state there were barely 500 miles of all-weather road. Acre is extremely isolated. Ninety-five percent of its territory is still covered in dense forest.

Because more than half the population of Acre lives in the forest, their chief concern is how to get about. The government is trying desperately to persuade some rich sponsor to provide the state with a road: the Road to the Pacific—another extravagant Amazonian dream. Acre sees this road as the answer to all its problems. No longer the poor relation, Acre pictures itself in the forefront of a highly profitable export trade to the Far East, sending large amounts of timber and beef to the Japanese. Never mind that huge sums will be needed to build and maintain it; never mind that it will require the bankrupt Peruvians next door to complete their share over the formidable barrier of the Andes; never mind that there isn't *actually* a Japanese market for Brazilian beef—which can be exported only after being processed, because of foot-and-mouth disease. Such realities are petty quibbles to the businessmen of Acre. They have rushed to buy up the land near the future road, anticipating huge profits as land values rise and envisaging spreading pastures full of sleek white cattle ready to make even greater fortunes for their owners.

While these hopes are being entertained by the pro-development lobby, the original inhabitants of the forest are uneasily facing the prospect of change. Of the two million deep forest dwellers, 140,000 are Indians. The rest are *caboclos*—people of mixed blood whose ancestors drifted into the region over the last 500 years. They settled along the rivers and intermarried with the Indians. They survive by hunting, fishing, doing a little slash-and-burn agriculture, and extracting forest products such as rubber, nuts, medicinal plants, and hearts of palm. As the forests shrink, the *caboclos'* chance for a good life, like that of the Indians, shrinks as well.

A third group of people who live in the forest areas and in the new towns on the frontier are the administrators, scientists, ecologists, churchpeople, and political activists. Some of them come from other parts of the country, and others are native to the region. All are involved to some extent in the development of the area; all are interested and concerned. But these are not the real people of the forest. They are there to initiate forces of change or to react against them, to administer law and order, to protect the lands from incursion by outsiders, or to chronicle the riches of the forest. They are there in the pursuit of justice or to lead people to God. They are there because the forest is there or because the people are there. They do not seek to live either by preserving the forest or by removing it. They have different agendas, and so they appear in this book as commentators. They help shed light on a complex and sometimes confusing scene. They are sometimes in a better position than the forest people to interpret what is going on.

Juliet and I had come to Amazônia to see for ourselves what it was like. We wanted to hear what the different groups had to say. It seems only right to start with the first people: the Indians.

3
INDIANS

One day when there are no trees left, the heavens will
fall, and all men will be destroyed.
                                    —Juruna Indian saying

We met José Kulina at the bishop's house in Rio Branco, the capital of Acre. He had come to discuss tribal business with the indigenous missionary council and was sitting on the grass outside, waiting. I would have guessed his age to be around fifty, but it's hard to tell with the forest Indians. He was short and slim, with glossy black hair cut in a heavy fringe. He wore jeans and a red shirt, a necklace of fine black and white beads, a digital watch with a black plastic strap, and brown shoes with no socks. He closed his eyes for a long moment and then began to speak, slowly and softly at first.

"What is left of us now? My people are few, but between us we have named every corner of this land. Today there are more Indian place names than Indians.

"We are the first people. For centuries we have hunted in these forests and fished in these rivers. Without us the white man could not have survived. We showed him how to live here. We showed him how to grow corn and manioc. We showed him how to build his house. We showed him how to sleep in a hammock. We shared with him our knowledge of the trees and fruits of the forests. We showed him how to hunt the animals and the birds and the fish.

"We know that the soil needs to rest. We are not like the settlers who come in here and cut everything. We clear small gardens and we plant our sweet potatoes and yams and manioc. Then we pull up the undergrowth and the weeds, and chop down the trees. Before the rains come we do the burning. Then we plant corn, cotton, beans, tobacco, and squash. We grow watermelon, papaya, and pineapple. We put in banana trees and medicinal plants which we can harvest after the soil is exhausted and we have moved the gardens.

"We hunt the animals of the forest for our food. We use darts to catch the birds high in the canopy, and poisonous vines to stun the fish in the river. Our favorite meat is monkey. Then peccary, tapir, capybara, and big birds. We keep no domestic animals, as the white man does. There are always animals in the forest.

"In the rains we stay close to home and prepare our gardens. In the dry season we visit the other villages, and we have our ceremonies and feasts. We make journeys to collect cane for our arrows, and Brazil nuts and honey. Everything we need comes from the forest. We use certain woods for building our houses and for making our bows, we use cane for our arrows, and palm leaves for thatching. We make our nets from fibers. For medicine we use all the parts of the tree: resin, sap, bark, leaves, roots, seeds, and fruit.

"We live differently from the white man. We do not keep things as you do. We have no need. When our gardens are exhausted or when the game moves away from the area, we move the village. But now that we are learning to like the things of the white man, our lives are changing. To buy the goods the white man sells, we must produce things ourselves, we must gather rubber or Brazil nuts, or grow coffee. And so we have less time for hunting, feasting, and growing our food. Before, we did not think of this thing—time. Now we see that we no longer have it.

"The white man invades our forests, he cuts our trees, he takes gold from our rivers. In the past our people died from slavery and disease, now we are dying because the white man is taking our lands. The ranchers try to seize them, the settlers invade them and the government confiscates them in order to put in big dams and new roads. They talk of moving us onto settlement schemes as if we were white men. But we are not white men. We do not own the land. We honor her, we use her, she is our mother.

"Now they tell us that they will demarcate our reserves so that nobody can take them from us. But they only talk and they do nothing, and we cannot prove that the lands are ours.

"We do not live as the white man lives. Our leaders are the ones who show themselves the best hunters and the wisest men. We do not compete with each other like you do. There is enough for everyone, we do not need to keep things for ourselves. Since we have learned to want the things of the white man, we see that we need things we did not know we needed. And to get these things we need money. We find that we are no longer equal. Some of us collect more things than others. Some of us want more things than others. And things are not like they were before."

Everyone knows that Christopher Columbus discovered America in 1492. The reason we know this is that history is written by the conquerors. But for the Indians, 1492 was the beginning of 500 years of defeat, domination, and death.

In 1637, a traveler in the Amazon described the people as "so numerous that if a dart were to fall from the air it would strike the head of an Indian." There were an estimated five million Indians in Brazil. Today there are 250,000 left. Of these, 140,000 still live in the Amazon, in varying stages of integration with the white world. There are probably still several uncontacted tribes, but their numbers must be small.

In general, the impact of white men on the Indians has been murderous, but things are starting to change. Although the record of the Federal Indian Authority, FUNAI, is mixed, there has been a lot of support at the national level from groups such as the Pro-Indian Commission and the militant wing of the Catholic church. Organizations such as Survival International and well-known foreigners such as the rock star Sting have brought the Indians to worldwide attention. The Indians themselves have formed associations to strengthen the ties between them, overcoming centuries of tribal rivalries and warfare. At last they are regaining self-confidence and pride; at last they are beginning to exercise political power. The Union of Indigenous Nations (UNI) is the forum where they discuss among themselves the issues they face.

We found our way, with some difficulty, to the UNI office in Rio Branco. It was a modest room in a modest quarter of town, furnished with a desk, a typewriter, a fan, and a few chairs. A number of Indians were wandering about. The leaders, all young men, politely offered chairs and were happy to talk to us. Toya Manchinere was the spokesperson. Short and powerfully built, with thick black hair, he was dressed in jeans, T-shirt, and athletic shoes. Some of his companions were reserved, and one glowered throughout, but Toya was open and smiling.

"Here in Acre and southern Amazonas there are about 9,000 Indians," he began. "We come from fifteen different nations. This is the Acre branch of UNI. Did you talk to our people down in São Paulo? Well, we don't always see eye to eye. They're in the city, and we feel that they're not really in touch with the Indians out in the villages. It's like this business of Sting and Raoni [the head of the Txucarramae tribe, who travels with Sting to publicize the plight of the Indians]. They got a lot of publicity and raised a lot of money. Set up a foundation in Brasília, with a nice air-conditioned office. But it hasn't done *us* any good. Not a single cent has come our way! [According to The Rainforest Foundation, it has spent more than $1 million on projects aiding indigenous communities in Brazil.]

"One of the things we're trying to do at UNI is to be a center of information about the Indians. We see ourselves as a link between our people and yours. Another thing we do is help our people to organize themselves. We've got to decide what we want, so we can ask the government to help us. One of the things we're working on now is the Indian Statute. I don't know if you've seen it? It's the law about the Indians. They say that Brazil has the best Indian laws of any country. It's just that they aren't respected! Well, the law is being revised, and the government has asked us for suggestions. So we are working on that. We've printed up a copy of the statute and we've added comments so that the people in the villages can understand it. We travel around as much as we can, so that we can discuss it with our people. We're trying to get their ideas on what sort of changes they want.

"For example, in Article 45 it says that the government can give the mining companies the right to come in and dig up minerals on our land. They say that the Indian Agency will make sure that our rights are respected. But we know that mining brings us nothing but harm. The pumping and drilling frighten off the game and kill the fish. The miners bring sickness and try to bribe us with presents and liquor.

"The government treats us like children. Well, they don't know it, but they've been raising the alligator's young! And now those young are full grown!

"They are always telling us that we need this or we need that, or we must think of a project and they will give us money. They want to give us money for things we don't ask for, for things we don't need. What we *do* need is time to think it all through, and then we can decide what we want.

"A lot of people come here to help the Indians. Fine. They think that deep in the forest everything is beautiful. Well, that isn't true. I would say that life in the villages is getting more and more difficult. We're under pressure from the military. Did you know that they've got a secret plan to move us onto small plots like settlers? They say it's something to do with securing the frontiers. But this is supposed to be a civilian government, isn't it? Then there are the settlers. They're after our lands. And the ranchers. They're after *everyone's* lands! And if the Pacific Road really gets built . . . well, we will just have to be ready."

Toya got to his feet, smiled, and helped himself to a cigarette from his friend Antonio Apurinã.

"You talk, Antonio," he commanded. "They've heard enough from me."

Antonio had been watching us closely while Toya was speaking. He flashed us a smile, looked at the floor for a time, and seemed to be collecting his thoughts.

"How can I explain it to you, this wrenching change that has come to my people? Some of us have only been in touch with the white man for twenty years, or less. Twenty years ago, we had nothing. But we had enough. And we were never sick. Now, suddenly, we have become people who need things. We eat your food. We wear your clothes. We use your tools, your guns, your radios and cassette recorders. We travel in your cars. We own things. But we cannot own all the things we want, because we do not have the money.

"Everything must change. We must produce things so that we can have the money to buy other things. The rhythm of our lives must change. We used to hunt when we were hungry, rest when we were tired, feast when we were happy. Now we eat your food, and we grow fat and lazy, and we are no longer strong like we used to be. Before, we were rich; now, we are poor.

"I left my village ten years ago. My father told me that I must learn your language so that I can understand your ways. He told me to know my enemy! He said that we can no longer live as we used to, that things will never again be as they were.

"To live in your world we need so many things. We need health programs because we are sick. We need schools because most of us can't read. And we need to be able to demarcate our lands. Otherwise we will never be safe from invaders. Of course most whites don't care about the Indians. All they care about is our land. The missionaries want our spirits, the ecologists want our forests, the loggers want our timber, the miners want our gold. And the anthropologists want to write clever books about us!

"But we want to speak for ourselves. We understand that we must change. We don't want to be zoo animals or museum pieces. We have to make our own place in your world, but we don't have to end up exactly like you. We must never forget who we are."

Later we talked to the national coordinator of UNI, Ailton Krenak. In his middle thirties, good-looking, supremely self-confident, he has become one of the chief Indian voices—both nationally and internationally. It was Ailton who appeared in a suit and tie to make a speech at the Congress in Brasília, and then slowly transformed himself into a forest Indian by painting his face with *genipapo* dye as he spoke. His flair for the dramatic is matched by his facility with words.

"In the indigenous cycle of things," he told us, "when we stayed too long in an area we would see that the game fled and that people's dreams were no longer good. So we would leave and let our houses collapse. But that place was not lost to us or abandoned, because sometimes we had our dead there, and we knew that we would always return. For this reason we would plant fruits, medicines, and magic plants for this life and for the other forest lives that would follow us. We saw that forest not as a wild bunch of trees but as a place in which our history and our future was written; the trees planted to remember the dead or to provide someday for our sons and daughters. The forest is not a wild thing to us, it is our world.

"We have lived in this place for a long time, a very long time, since the time when the world did not yet have this shape. We learned with the ancients that we are a tiny part of this immense universe—fellow travelers with all the animals, the plants, and the water. We are a part of the whole, we cannot hurt or destroy our home. Now we want to talk to those who cannot yet manage to see the world in this way; to say to them that together we have to take care of this boat in which we are all sailing."

After talking to Indians in the towns, we felt that it was time to visit the villages. Our chance came when we met Maria Barcelos. Maria runs a health project with the Suruí Indians of Rondônia. Dark and gypsy-like, she has a wild mass of hair and wears a lot of Indian jewelry. Maria is highly unusual in acknowledging her Indian blood. She claims to have a Xavante grandmother and likes to be known as Maria *dos indios*—Maria of the Indians.

"Yes, you can come with me to the reserve," she said, a little grudgingly. "But you'll be coming as my friends, not as tourists. So don't try and take any pictures, and it's better if you let me do the talking."

Like many others we were to meet, Maria was fiercely protective of her adopted tribe.

"Let me tell you a little bit about the Suruí. They were only contacted just over twenty years ago. They had a pretty tough introduction to the white world, because the government put in a settlement scheme right next to where they live. In fact their lands were invaded by a bunch of squatters in 1976, and there was a terrific fight. It was FUNAI who saved the day. They told the settlers they'd have to leave as soon as they had harvested their crops. Well, the settlers had planted some coffee, and the Suruí decided to take it over. At first they thought it would be a good idea, because they could sell the coffee and buy what they wanted from the whites. What they didn't know was how much work it takes to grow coffee. They found that they didn't have enough time to go hunting and collecting food from the forest. The price of coffee went down. But by that time they were accustomed to eating white man's food and had to find other ways of making money. So they started to sell some of the timber off the reserve.

"They did receive some goods in exchange, but they were always being cheated, and they couldn't do anything about it because they didn't know how to read and write, and they couldn't count up to more than ten anyway. There was a lot of trouble about the distribution of the goods as well, because the chiefs didn't know how to parcel them out without causing friction. So the Suruí ended up worse off than before, and now they want to find some other way of making money.

"They call themselves the *Paiter*, which means the People. They're divided into two groups, the forest people and the harvest people. The forest people are the hunters and the gatherers. The harvest people grow corn, manioc, potatoes, yams, cotton, peanuts, and tobacco.

"Every few years the harvest people give a big feast for the whole tribe. This is a time of great rejoicing when everyone drinks a great deal of *chicha* [corn beer] and gets wildly drunk. The forest people bring presents of necklaces, hammocks, feathers, baskets, bows, and arrows as their contribution. For some years they stopped having this feast, but now they've started again, and I think that's a sign that the tribe is beginning to adjust to the new ways.

"There's so much we can learn from the Indians. For one thing, they're all equal. The only ones who are different are the *caciques*—the chiefs—and the *pajé*—the medicine man. When they go to the fields, the whole family goes together. It's a hard job, clearing the forest, so the women go too, to support their men. They know that sharing work makes it easier. They also know that there is a time for being lazy, although even when they are lying in their hammocks they're never idle; they're always making baskets or arrows, or something."

To get to the reserve, we had to drive along miles of bone-shaking dirt roads, through a straggling settlement scheme with its small wooden houses, fields of corn, beans, and vegetables, and large areas of abandoned pasture.

It was a relief to enter the cool forest, although the road soon ran out altogether, and we had to enter the reserve on foot. Around the corner an abandoned FUNAI pickup truck was sitting in the middle of the road. One of its wheels had been removed, and it looked as though it had been neglected for a long time. "See that?" gestured Maria. "Been there for months. No money to buy another tire. Can't expect them to do much if they don't even have the money for a tire!"

The village was wrapped in silence. The men of the forest were hunting. Some of the others had traveled, improbably enough, almost 2,500 miles to Rio de Janeiro to take part in a rock concert with a famous samba singer. Inside the dark wooden huts the women were busily preparing food. In a small central building, manioc roots were being scraped and grated. There was a pile of rusty sardine tins in one corner. Dogs were scratching themselves in the sun, babies were rolling in the dust, and a donkey galloping through the village caused no one any surprise.

In one corner of the FUNAI post was a small dispensary where a young nurse, paid for by Maria's project, was looking at a couple of snuffly children. A bunch of kids came giggling through the forest—the first shift back from school. They looked healthy and happy.

At one end of the village stood a solitary *maloca*, the traditional-style house. It looked like an upside-down basket, with palm thatch walls to the ground. Maria told us that the *malocas* are always cool and bug-free. Inside were a few hammocks, a pile of clothes, and a transistor radio—nothing exotic.

The next village was some miles away through the forest. Here the health clinic was housed in a smart new building. It was capably run by blonde Mariana, a settler's daughter married to a Suruí.

She showed us the big *maloca* where the village holds its ceremonies, pointing to the hollowed-out tree trunks where the corn beer is kept. On the walls hung a collection of baskets, armadillo shells, rifles, and bows and arrows. The Suruí had built small fires underneath the hammocks, and the *maloca* was lit by the village generator, connected up with fencing wire.

Mariana took us along a forest path to visit her house. It was made of saplings, with a wood-shingled roof. No one was living there at the moment, she explained. Her husband was away in the lands of the Cinta Larga; her children were being looked after by their grandmother.

"I sleep in the clinic at night," she added. "Because of the Cabeça Seca."

The Cabeça Seca, she told us, was a spirit sent by their enemies, the Zoró, to frighten them. It walks through the dark with a flare, and it comes up to the *malocas* and bangs on the walls. Nobody goes outside after nightfall if they can help it.

Back in the village, we were offered lemonade and roasted manioc in one of the *malocas*. We flopped into hammocks to listen to a discussion about the timber problem.

"It was FUNAI who suggested we sell our mahogany," said Enrique, one of the younger leaders of the tribe. "They said they had no money to give us, and that we'd better find ways of making our own. Well, the whole business has split the tribe from one end to another. Worse yet, outsiders began to get involved. They were only trying to help. A couple of priests denounced the loggers and said they were cheating us, which of course they were. Well, one of the priests got shot dead.

"The logging continues, but it hasn't benefited the tribe as a whole. One or two people have done all right, but most of us don't even realize what is going on. We're not used to thinking about owning things, you see. But we're going to have to do something about the logging, or we'll wake up one day and find that all the mahogany has gone, and all we have to show for it is a miserable little generator, a second-hand pickup truck, and a few bottles of liquor."

The issue for the Indians is harsh but simple: extinction or integration. They face extinction because their lands are coveted by so many others in the area. And when these others come, they bring the white man's diseases, which the Indians—having no immunity—often die from. The loggers destroy the forest, and the game vanishes. The gold miners poison the waters with mercury, and the fish become contaminated. The Indians face extinction as they become detribalized and disheartened and seek a cure for their unhappiness in apathy and alcohol. They face extinction because sometimes they cannot make the sudden violent jump from the Stone Age into the twentieth century, and they kill themselves or their children out of despair.

The alternative is integration. But how exactly is this to be done? Must they become *caboclos*, like their half-caste cousins? Will they be able to retain their Indianness? Or, as Ailton Krenak says, will their dreams no longer be good? Will they have the courage to choose from the white man's world and resist what does not feel right for them?

They will not have the luxury of time to think about these things unless they first attend to the urgent problem of their lands. These lands are coveted by just about everybody. To the

whites it seems unfair that a small number of Indians should pos-
sess so large an area of land. So they invade. They come for the
timber, or the gold, or the land itself. Sometimes the Indians and
the invaders fall into bloody conflict, as in the case of the coloniz-
ers and the Suruí. Sometimes the Indians raid settlements and
take things from the whites. Sometimes they steal children.
Sometimes they kill.

To the government, the Indians are an embarrassment. There is
little sympathy in Brasília for people like Sting who go around
giving Brazil bad publicity. The government also faces a dilemma.
Large areas of Amazônia, with all its economic potential, are
claimed by a tiny number of Indians. Thanks to a combination of
collective bad conscience and national and international pressure,
provision must be made for these Indians. However, there are
huge numbers of other Brazilian citizens with pressing needs. One
way to attend to these needs is to draw on the bank account called
Amazônia by developing the region with roads and towns and
dams and agriculture. But development will surely lead to clashes
with the forest people.

Decisions were easier to make in the days of the generals. They
would simply have had the Indians moved out of the frontier
zones—on the excuse of strengthening security—and settled on
small plots of land. Fortunately for the Indians, the military is no
longer in power.

In November 1991, then-President Collor's government was
hailed internationally for demarcating reserves for the Yanomami
and the Mencragnotire Kayapó. Presently the Yanomami's land
rights to 23.5 million acres and the Mencragnotire's to nearly 12.3
million acres have been officially recognized. The Indians, however, do not have rights to the subsoil (that is, to minerals). Overall
the Indians now have the rights to 42 million of the 220 million
acres that they claim.

Many people see this as belated justice. Others question the
fairness of allocating almost 2,500 acres per head to some Brazilian
citizens while millions of others have no land at all.

There have long been conflicting views of the Indians. Some
see them as victims of the white man's greed and rapacity; others
see them as the keepers of the forest and its secrets. The *caboclos*,
who have shared the forest for centuries and who owe their

knowledge of its ways to the Indians, still regard them as little better than animals. Others see them as innocents, ripe for exploitation. They give them cans of sardines, radios, corn spirit, and cocaine so that they will become addicted to white man's things and sell their timber for nothing.

But all is not gloom and doom for the beleaguered Indians. They have found their own voice and are starting to speak out about their future. In 1989 they scored a notable victory by overturning the clause in the Indian Statute that defined them as wards of the state. The alligator's child has indeed grown.

The Indians have aligned themselves with the rubber tappers and the river people to form the Alliance of the Forest Peoples. They are campaigning vigorously for recognition and demarcation of their lands, and they insist on taking part in government discussions of all projects taking place on their lands.

The Indians don't want to live in someone else's forest fairy tale. Like the rest of us, they want to see their lives and their children's lives improve. Darrell Posey, an anthropologist working with the Kayapó, points out that, like everyone else, they will make good choices and bad ones. They know what they want. They want access to health and education facilities. They would like assistance with marketing and credit. They would like compensation for their knowledge of forest products, notably medicines. They point out that drug companies use Indian knowledge and pocket the profits themselves.

The white man has done and still does incalculable harm to the Indian, but these days the future is beginning to look a little brighter. After an initial disastrous decline, the number of Indians is beginning to increase. Although some groups still verge on extinction, others show strong signs of recovery. Natshi Suruí, a high school student, told us how he felt about the two worlds. "I was educated outside the village," he said, "and I understand the ways of the white man. But they are not my ways, and your world is not my world. I will take many things back to the village, things that I have learned in your world. And my life can never be like that of my father. But my people must make their own way, and I wish to be there to help them."

4

LOGGERS

The gods are mighty, but mightier still is the forest.
—Indian saying

The early sunlight filters through the misty morning. Across the muddy river, a little patch of straggly forest appears, and suddenly an *ipé* tree blazes brilliant yellow against the murky background. Howler monkeys salute the morning. A scarlet and black tanager perches in a banana tree. A neat black and white "washerwoman" bird skims across the river. From the bridge that carries the BR-364—the road that has brought life to Rondônia and destruction to the forest and its inhabitants— comes a subdued roar of trucks.

We are in one of those sprawling new towns that has grown from almost nothing in fifteen years. Now the population is close to 50,000, but the place remains a straggling collection of wooden shacks. It has a temporary feel to it, and it looks like someone is still thinking about building a proper town. Everything is far away from everything else, linked by roads that unexpectedly wander off into the bush as little muddy tracks.

Long lines of great tarpaulin-covered trucks inch along, feeling their way over speed-breakers like a procession of dinosaurs. Your glance automatically turns to the road. You feel that you are on the way to something, but you can't be sure what it is.

On the edge of town lies the sawmill. In the yard there are mammoth stacks of mahogany logs, each with a girth as great as a man's height. The big logs get fed into a mechanical saw and sliced sideways, like cheese. Three men in flip-flops and work gloves casually manage the huge carcasses.

The sliced wood is carefully placed on trolleys and laid flat, to be swiftly sawn into planks. The offcuts lie untidily about—so much good wood wasted. The piles of burning waste send up aromatic smoke that mingles with the gray pall that hangs over the landscape. It is the burning season.

The mill owner wanders over, hitching up his shorts beneath his belly. "You want to know where this stuff comes from? It comes from the Suruí Indians. They've got plenty more in there. I get their wood. The chief gets a pickup truck and a parabolic antenna for his television. Everyone's happy.

"These forests were given to us by God to be used. I go in there, I get out the good trees, I move on. Now there's a lot of trees that are fine timbers, but they're not known outside Amazônia. So there's really no market for them. It's a pity really. A waste, you might say. The international market works only with the few woods it knows—cedar, mahogany, jacaranda, cerejeira, virola.

"Take rosewood now. That's nearly all gone. But there's at least ten or fifteen types of wood that we could be exporting. Somebody ought to be creating a market for them. But that's not my job. My job is to get those trees out. And the good stuff is getting harder to find.

"Mind you, there's some countries where they want to ban the import of tropical hardwoods altogether. The ones that are endangered, that is. Can you imagine anything so silly? Do that, and there'll be no point having forests at all. After all, if they're worth something, people will take the trouble to look after them.

"Not that the ranchers bothered when they came in and started clearing the land. Shameful the way they set fire to all that good timber. They say they lost hundreds of millions of dollars worth of wood on those ranches that the government backed with all that money. As for the hydro schemes! Do you know who got the concession for clearing the timber at the Tucuruí dam? The military government gave it to those jokers from CAPEMI! And you know who they are, don't you? They run a military pension scheme, that's who they are. It's obvious that *they* couldn't handle something like that. Cronyism, that's what it was, giving the job to those people. What do you expect *them* to know about logging?

They lost a fortune in good timber in there.

"Do you know what happened then? The CAPEMI boys couldn't get the timber out, so the electricity company went ahead and flooded the area anyway. Then they discovered that the trees were rotting and the turbines were rusting out. They had to send people in to cut the wood with underwater saws. Did you ever hear anything so ridiculous? Stupid is what I call it.

"Of course we've got to make roads before we can get the trees out. And once those roads are there we have to keep a sharp look-out, otherwise the place will be crawling with little men with chain saws. You wouldn't believe how quickly they'll be in there, if you give them half a chance. And *they're* followed by the settlers going in there to plant their manioc. Well, they can do what they like after I've finished. I don't care *what* they do. But if they get under my feet. . . . Still, I got ways of taking care of them."

He hitched up his shorts once more and gave me a wink that combined lewdness and menace to such an extent that I instinctively stepped back out of reach. "Anyway," he continued, grinning at my discomfiture, "we got to make these roads, and we got to get our machines in there. The good woods, sometimes there's not more than a handful of them in several acres. It's a lot of work, let me tell you. And we've got to get in and out of there while the weather holds up.

"This mill belongs to me and my dad. We've been here almost as long as the town itself; sixteen years ago we started up. The place looked very different then, I can tell you. We aren't allowed to export whole logs, so we process them here. If our technology was a bit more advanced we wouldn't be wasting so much good wood.

"But we haven't got the machinery, we can't get the parts, and we're always having problems with maintenance. And we don't have the infrastructure. You know what the situation is with the electricity. Atrocious, that's what it is. And it isn't easy to keep good workers when you *can* find them. These people never stick to anything for long. I suppose that's what comes from being a state of immigrants.

"This business of using only a few species puts a lot of pressure on the ones people like. That means they're getting scarcer. And all those other good woods are just going to waste. We have to keep the volume up, that's the only way we can make ends meet in this business. Not that it's a bad business, as businesses go in this crazy place. I'd say that the outlook is excellent, if the government doesn't keep butting in. Down in the south they've chopped down all their forest, so wood is beginning to get quite scarce in some places. Of course you've got to look at the economics of the thing. I mean, there's always going to be a demand. But sometimes you get a rancher and he tells you he's got some good wood, but you just can't get in there. If you haven't got the quantity and you haven't got the access, you might as well save yourself the trouble. It just isn't worth the effort.

"No, reforestation isn't my business. When I'm through, the landowner will go in there and burn the place over, and then he'll turn it into pasture. He can't afford to even think of reforesting. He's not going to be around in fifty years when those trees come in. Mind you, there *are* a few people looking into the question. It ought to be done. But it's not my job. We've got to look after ourselves here and now, haven't we?"

Think reforestation, and you've got to think of Nick Burch. Start talking loggers, and his name is bound to crop up.

"He's some crazy Englishman planting mahogany in Rondônia."

"They say he's gone bust this time."

"Last time I was there, he was hiding from his creditors in a canoe downriver."

"You must look up Nick. He's a rough diamond, but he knows his stuff."

Nick lives in an elegant wooden house on the edge of a large muddy river. "Built it myself," he says, as he shows us around. Inside, everything is exquisitely crafted—floors, walls, ceilings, furniture—all made of beautiful hardwoods. Here is someone who knows and loves wood.

Nick, at thirty-eight, is blond, bulky, and red-faced. Thoroughly macho, he likes to demonstrate his fitness by standing on his head and doing push-ups. These days he's running to fat. "Not as fit as I was," he says, happily stowing away another beer, the umpteenth of the day. He tells us that he used to be a champion boxer, and he's still pretty handy with his fists. He's a Cockney, but the accent comes and goes. He doesn't speak English much these days. From what he tells us—and he talks nonstop— he leads a colorful life. He once had three death threats in a single week. "So long as they come close, you can deal with them," he remarked. "The real danger is if they try to shoot from a distance." He thinks that no one will actually do him in. "They don't want another Chico Mendes."

At least one of the death threats was connected with the Surui wood. Nick had evidence that one of the local loggers had been robbing the Surui. "Look at these," he said, gesturing at a pile of receipts. "Look at the number of logs they claim to have taken out in one load! Seventeen! You can't fit more than four or five on a truck, and if you *really* took seventeen you'd be cutting them way too small. That's illegal too." Rumor has it that Nick himself has been involved in taking trees from the Surui, but he didn't go into that. He did display an almost paternalistic attitude toward them. "Sure I work with them. At one stage I used to pay for a doctor to go into the reserve, since the government agency couldn't afford to do so. I gave them a generator. And I'm doing some reforestation for them."

Nick's current passion, which is costing him dearly, is what he describes as "the most important reforestry project in South America." He is not only reforesting his own land, but is also working with a group of settlers as well as the Surui. He has bankrolled these projects himself, and they have nearly done him in. At one stage the cash flow was so low that the phone, water, and electricity were all cut off. None of this fazed Nick. He used someone else's fax machine, he illegally reconnected the water, he installed a diesel generator, and he was getting fuel on credit. "I've sold off everything I could," he pointed out. "I must pay the wages somehow."

Nick employs fifty people in the nurseries, and he runs the administration, rather haphazardly, with his son, Jason. But the financial support he had been counting on hasn't materialized. Recently money has been so tight that he hasn't been able to plant a lot of his seedlings, which means that they'll die when the dry season comes along. "I haven't got support from anybody," he says in an aggrieved tone. "I mean, this Polonoroeste project that they had here in the state. There was $10 million in there for forestry projects. The forestry people haven't planted a *single* tree! They're all crooked, and I'm not afraid to tell them so. Of course nobody believes me when I say that, but take a look here in the paper. The two top men have been charged with incompetence and corruption. See what I mean? All that money for planting trees, and the only one actually putting the trees in the ground—that's me—is practically bankrupt.

"As for the professional foresters from places like the World Bank, they're not much better. They sit in five-star hotels doing flog-all and skimming off the cash. Then they go home and write another bloody report. I used to worry that all the trees in the jungle would be cut down to make paper for their reports on how to save the rain forest!"

Nick collects women and children with Tudor prodigality. In fact there's something about him reminiscent of Henry VIII. He fathered his first child at fifteen. "I always say that a man must do three things in life. Plant a tree, father a child, and write a book. Well, I've written books. Not that anyone is interested in them. And I've fathered enough children. Now I'm planting trees.

"I've knocked around a lot in my time. I worked in forestry in the south of England. Then I got interested in tropical woods, so I came to Brazil to take a look at the mahogany. Well, I liked it so much I decided to stick around. Then it occurred to me that if someone didn't do something about reforestry, there wouldn't be any mahogany left. So I got involved. Ten years I've been in Rondônia—longer than I've ever lived anywhere. I consider myself a Rondônian. I love it here. Don't reckon I'll be going anywhere else now.

"I've made a lot of money in my time, you know. And lost it. I once ran a business selling furniture made right here in town. I used to send it to England. And I work with Brazil nuts. Last year I handled most of the nut harvest in the country. I'm interested in getting back into the furniture business. Reckon I'll make parts, components. Like tabletops for pubs, that sort of thing. Good way of using up the offcuts. And it'll provide employment."

Nick becomes very serious when he's talking forestry or, better still, when he's out there actually showing you. His right-hand man is a darkly bearded woodsman from Paraná who looks like Davy Crockett. "This is Daví. Best bloody woodsman in South

America." Daví squints out from beneath the brim of his battered hat, emitting a thick cloud of smoke from the cheapest and nastiest cigarette available. "People think he's my gunman!" laughs Nick. He looks as though he could be.

After a quick tour of the nursery it's time to go to the forest. A corrugated dirt road runs through dense *capoeira* scrub and skeletons of burnt trees—a ruined landscape under the smoky sky. We go through a rickety gate and along a rough track to reach one of Nick's trial reforestry areas. This plot is situated in an area of secondary forest. Nick has opened up corridors and planted them with hardwoods—mahogany and cedar. Daví gestures towards a single two-year-old mahogany, already over ten feet high. Some of the young trees are suffering from borer beetles, but he doesn't seem concerned. By planting in corridors, Nick explains, they are getting as close as possible to the natural growth of primary forest.

"I'm interested in planting mixed stands of trees, including fruit trees and rubber," Nick continues. "I've planted over 200,000 seedlings, you know, from thirty species. What we have to figure out is how to make these forests too valuable to burn down. It's not as if we need more agricultural land anyway. What we need is better technology.

"One of my ideas is to select a plot of land, say 250 acres, and contract with the landowner for fifty percent of the value of the commercial products produced over a period of, say, thirty years. We'd do the reforesting and manage the place. I'd like to prove that properly harvested forest can yield far higher returns than land cleared for agriculture or raising cattle. You start with mixed agroforestry, including some subsistence crops, and as you go along you plant more valuable species so that the value of the land increases—instead of mining the land and leaving it fit for nothing. I'm working with the rubber tappers too on different small projects. Those involve proper management of the rubber trees, something that's never been done. And replanting, of course. Not only rubber trees but other things that you can harvest, like fruit trees and plants for oils and essences.

"I'd like to get into replanting at the mining sites over at Bom Futuro. The laws are quite strict, but what they did down in Minas Gerais, for example, was nothing more than putting the place under eucalyptus. I'd like to work with mixed forest and see if we can't create an area that can be sustainably managed. And another thing; I want to work with those abandoned pastures. That land could be put to productive use, even if it never goes back to forest."

Racing back to town to meet some deadline, Nick stops off for a couple of glasses of cane spirit in the only roadside bar for miles around. Outside, there's a burned-out skeleton of a truck cab; inside, a pool table and an elderly freezer stocked with beer. It's thirsty weather. The smoky air catches you in the back of the throat.

"Daví's a good bloke," said Nick, putting his arm affectionately around his friend's shoulder. "Never will accept a salary, you know. I give him money when he needs it. He gets offended when I try and offer him a regular wage. People think I'm exploiting him. A load of balls. What I say is this. As long as I'm running the most important reforestry project in South America entirely out of my own pocket, I can do as I bloody well like."

Nick is a rarity among the loggers; he is one of the few who is able to look even slightly further than immediate profits. But he has gone bust. "That doesn't invalidate my theories," he says with engaging frankness. "There are two reasons for that. First, I was naive enough to believe that the money that had been promised me by various donors would actually materialize—which it didn't. If I'd known that, I'd have committed my funds differently and continued with the logging in order to finance the reforestry. Secondly, I should have had a good administrator. I'm no good at that sort of thing. It doesn't interest me. If I'd had somebody overseeing the thing, I could have done something before I got into serious trouble. And they could have written up the project proposals for me."

Forestry requires a time scale that is totally outside our way of thinking. Even in the tropics, where everything grows at high speed, today's planter of hardwoods is unlikely to be around to harvest them in forty or fifty or seventy years' time. Similarly, if a government sets up a rational forestry policy, it will not itself be able to see the benefits of that policy.

Brazil has a highly sophisticated forest code—except that it doesn't work. If a government can't enforce its own legislation, it needs to find sweeteners to persuade people to regulate their own behavior. Most of the logging in the Amazon takes place on private lands, so it's the landowners who must be persuaded to manage their forestlands sustainably.

Current legislation works against this. A higher value is placed on cleared land than on forestland. And the very act of clearing, which is regarded as an improvement, helps reinforce the validity of land claims. Now that it's obvious that large ranching schemes won't work in the Amazon, the government should remove the remaining financial support from them and channel the money into sensible programs of forest management. In addition, cleared land that is unproductive should be considered less valuable than forestland. Let the settlers clear enough forest to grow their crops, and show them how to use the land more productively. Then they won't need to clear any more.

From the loggers' point of view, their best bet is to cut and run. Markets are uncertain, the currency fluctuates wildly, and the country's economic stability is nonexistent. Always, at the back of their minds, is the feeling that the government may change the rules of the game overnight. They may even get caught on one of their frequent clandestine incursions onto Indian and forest reserves. There's no incentive to think beyond tomorrow.

Brazil has always been plagued by such predatory short-term thinking. Brazilian history repeats itself in a series of booms and busts—typical of a country with lots of space and abundant resources. The prevailing attitude has been "There's plenty more where that comes from." One crop or commodity after another is gaily exploited. Brazil has lived through cycles of sugar, cocoa, gold, rubber, coffee, and now timber. Each has brought a short boom, followed by a bust.

I asked one of the lumber dealers in Nick's town if he had any suggestions for more efficient logging. As he handed me a cup of sweet dark coffee, he said, "You want to know what we *are* doing in Rondônia, or what we *should* be doing? There's two aspects of it, for those of us who are involved in the wood trade. First there's the question of getting the timber out of the forest. Then there's the business of processing it.

"I run a mill, so I need access to a good steady supply of lumber. That's one reason why I cut it myself. Mind you, I buy it from others as well, but if I didn't have my own cutting operation I'd never be able to rely on anything. You see, we have two seasons here in Rondônia. In the wet season—that's from December to April—the whole place turns into a quagmire. The local roads are bad enough, but the logging roads are out of the question! That means there's five months with no lumber coming in. And if I didn't have good storage facilities, I'd have to close down. Lots of the smaller operations do just that. At least I can keep going year-round. That much I *can* control.

"And I have my own power plant. No use relying on those clowns from CERON [the Rondônia Electric Company] to come up with any decent power supply. The only people in this state who get any regular electricity are the politicians. You've seen what it's like. The power's off more than it's on.

"I look after my boys—pay them a fair wage and treat them real good. But it's not easy to keep them on the job once planting season starts. There's always a shortage of skilled labor, but it's not worth my while to train them—not if they just keep running off.

"What *could* I be doing? I could be installing better equipment, that's what. Right now I'm reluctant to commit too many resources to modernizing the mill. You know the economic situation in this place. But if the government were to demonstrate some really solid support—credits and that sort of thing—I'd be happy to update a bit.

"If I could get some good machinery, and if I felt I could rely on a regular supply of spares and decent maintenance people, do you know what I'd do? I'd set up a little furniture business. Start with the local market, then maybe expand into the national market. Who knows? I might even be able to sell the stuff abroad. 'Save the rain forest. Buy genuine Amazon mahogany furniture made by local craftsmen.' That might go down well, don't you think? I could go into wood flooring too. There's lots of demand for that.

"Plywood, that's another thing. Did you know that most of our hardwood that goes to Japan is made into plywood? Well to me that seems a waste of good wood. If we could produce our own plywood, it would have to be resistant to fire, damp, and insect damage—real quality stuff—then we could fill that niche in the market, and the good timbers could be used for making veneer and fine furniture. I mean, we've got a good product here. We ought to be figuring out ways to use it properly."

For ideas on forest management, we went to talk to the foresters at FUNTAC, the state environmental agency and research center in the neighboring state of Acre.

FUNTAC is a long bus ride out of the center of town. The bus leaves us on the edge of a broad road in the middle of what will one day be an industrial estate. For now, it's just a collection of warehouses and fading signs announcing future construction and manufacturing projects. But when we locate FUNTAC (a complex of handsome wooden buildings linked by boardwalks), our spirits rise. A lot goes on in FUNTAC, and it receives substantial injections of foreign funding for its many projects. The researchers are investigating the properties of lesser-known woods, doing an ecological zoning project using Landsat satellite pictures, and studying hydrography, soils, ethnobotany, better ways of processing forest products, and ways of implanting agroforestry systems in local communities. We spoke to the senior forester—a slight, dark, soft-spoken man—in his office, which was littered with soil samples in plastic bags and had tree seedlings propped against the walls. He told us what he thought should be done.

"There's a lot of agitation in Europe and the United States these days about banning imports of all but sustainably produced timber. Well, that cuts out the Amazon right there. There just isn't any timber being produced sustainably in the Amazon at this point. So, room for improvement? There certainly is. It's in the hands of the government really.

"One thing we Brazilians haven't given nearly enough thought to is protecting the high quality of the woods. We'll have to get on much faster with better forest management and genetic improvement of our stock in order to conserve our fine timbers. We're doing a bit here and there but, as you know, foresters are treated like poor relations by other government departments.

"Education, that's the next thing. We've got to change people's attitudes. It *can* be done—look at what they did in Europe with those antismoking campaigns and all the stuff about drunk driving and the whole ecology bit. We've got to educate people to think differently about the forest. The Indians and the *caboclos*, they're at home in the forest. They treat it right, and they know how to make it work for them. But take the settlers. That includes almost the entire population of Rondônia, although there aren't so many here in Acre. Most of them came from the south. They came up here as pioneers. They saw the forest as an enemy to be conquered. The loggers saw it as a resource to be mined. The ranchers saw it as an obstruction to be removed. We've got to get people to see it as a valuable resource, not as a damned nuisance.

"We need a campaign of education. We could start with the forestry department, training its staff. What it's doing at the moment is persecuting the little guys for cutting down a tree here and there, when it ought to be after the big boys. It ought to be checking that the Indians get a fair deal if they insist on selling their wood. We ought to make sure that the forestry people get a decent salary, so that they're not so susceptible to looking the other way when they see people breaking the rules.

"We need to educate the schoolchildren and the settlers. Ranchers too, and people in towns. We should be using radio and television and the newspapers to show people how they can live well if they work *with* the ecosystem, not *against* it.

"The government is losing huge amounts of money on forestry. After all, it's one of the biggest money earners in the state. The government should be charging realistic stumpage fees. At the moment it's charging seventy-two cents U.S. a cubic meter, and most of that goes for administrative costs. It's supposed to be for reforestry, but that doesn't happen! As for the export taxes, they should be *much* higher. They should reflect the real value of the logs in environmental terms. There's going to be more and more demand for Amazon timber as the supplies in Asia and Africa run down. If we can get the timber exports on a good footing now, then we'll have something that's going to increase in value for years and years.

"Of course one of the best ways to change attitudes is by supplying cash bribes. Fiscal incentives, they call them. It's all the same thing! Instead of paying ranchers to clear huge chunks of forestland and subsidizing a whole lot of unprofitable settlement schemes, the government should be paying people to keep their land under forest and start replanting on the degraded lands. They could make money off it straight away by planting manioc, banana trees, fruit trees, coffee, cocoa, fuelwood, and fodder trees. Plantation crops, *guaraná*, oil palm, and hearts of palm would pay off in the slightly longer term, and then hardwoods. If we had a serious hardwood replanting program, then in a few decades we'd be able to supply all the world requirements for tropical timber without disturbing any more of the pristine forest. And we could keep our genetic reserves intact. They're going to be even more valuable to us than the timber.

"How are we going to finance all this? Well, we could provide tax breaks for forestry schemes. We could be hitting people hard who are clearing their land for unprofitable projects like cattle ranching. We've got to charge realistic logging fees. And we have to use some of this money to *prove* to the farmers that they can make a go of agroforestry. They'll need lots of support: seedlings, fertilizers, and help from the extension boys. We've got some projects going already in the settlement schemes and with the rubber tappers. We show them how to work with trees. They've got no experience, but they're beginning to see how they can make a profit out of it, and that's the best incentive of all!

"There's plenty of international funding available right now. Particularly with the Earth Summit conference just around the corner. We've got to cash in on all the interest. It's our big chance. After all, forestry doesn't mean keeping the place as a museum and not touching a tree. We've got the lion's share of the rain forest here in Brazil. If we can figure out a way to manage our forests really well, then we're on to a big winner."

5

RIVER PEOPLE

Rivers are highways that move on and bear us where
we wish to go.

—Blaise Pascal, 1662

Both the Indians and the loggers had been high-profile cases. Now it was time to consider some of the regular people of Amazônia—people who aren't making news but are living quietly as they have always lived. So Juliet and I took a friend's advice and booked passage to a small river town ten hours from Porto Velho.

We traveled on the "Orlandina." A neat little boat, its lower deck was piled high with cargo and stank of engine fumes; its top deck was a multicolored swirl of hammocks, with small children and bundles everywhere. We pulled out onto the broad muddy river, past distant houses on the shore. Perched high on stilts, each was surrounded by a plot of burnt land, wisps of smoke curling up in the afternoon sun.

We arrived in Calama at night. A flight of wooden steps led up into the darkness. Far above a few lights were twinkling. We made our way across the narrow gangplank and puffed up the stairs. At the top we found a grassy street with wooden houses. We made our way to the hotel—a small hot bunkhouse with an evil-smelling lavatory and mosquitoes.

Six a.m. on the riverfront: The cocks are crowing and the clean-up crew is on duty—a band of small black vultures prowling about investigating everything. There's no sign of anyone else.

34

Even the dogs are asleep.

The first stirrings of life: A canoe sweeps past. A man appears with a battered black Bible and a torch. Parrots fly overhead. It is a soft morning, slightly misty.

A tug propelling a barge inches around a bend in the river. A canoe with a nonfunctional outboard is poled into shore. The trucks on the barge catch the first rays of the sun. An engine starts up from the floating workshop/filling station at the foot of the steps. A motorboat streaks across the river.

A small boy carefully balances a large basket of bread as he heads down the steps. In the river the first dolphins surface, gray and pink.

On the riverfront an impressive wooden building houses the town generator. It is turned on from midday to midnight, a modest but reliable supply. Outside the generator house a large shady tree serves as the town notice board. Someone is offering cheap cane spirit at $1 a bottle. Another notice displays a list of bad debtors. Careca (Baldy). Beleza (Beauty). Alto (Lofty). They owe money for school supplies, jeans, tennis shoes, and liquor.

Breakfast in the hotel is served in the owner's kitchen next door: bread and eggs, sweet coffee with milk. The place houses a floating population. Today there is one very pregnant woman with an untreated case of malaria. One ancient woman, accompanied by a granddaughter, has come from a distant river to see the nurse. A girl is visiting from Humaitá, four hours downriver. Another girl with a pure Indian face, perhaps fourteen years old, has a new baby. There is no sign of a husband.

Dona Morena, the hotel owner, like many Amazonian women, is a large, handsome figure. She has, it turns out, a heart of gold.

"Go and talk to the schoolteachers," she advises. "They can tell you a lot about the town. They're always asking questions and trying to find out things. I think they're writing a report or something."

We head along the riverfront, across a narrow wooden footbridge. Far below, a riverboat lies stranded. At the school, which is shabby but well-kept, we meet Tyer. He is not a Rondônian; he comes from Ceará in the distant northeast, but there's a long tradition of his countrymen coming to Amazônia. Indeed, most Amazônians, river people, *caboclos*—whatever you call them— have Cearense blood in their veins.

"The people of Calama are the true Amazônians," he begins. "Their ancestors have been living along these rivers for hundreds of years. They call themselves whites, but they owe a lot more to the Indians than they'd care to admit! The first arrivals took Indian women, and they learned how to live in the Indian way. They build their houses on stilts to keep them above the floodwater. They sleep in hammocks. They grow their food like the Indians—clearing little plots in the forest and burning the weeds. The Indians showed them how to grow manioc, which is the staple diet in these parts, and how to process it. They taught them how to use forest plants for food and medicine and how to hunt and fish.

"They live today pretty much like they always did. They're basically extractors. They grow subsistence crops on the *várzeas*—the floodplains—and they hunt and fish and sometimes tap rubber or collect other forest products, like *copaíba* oil. They'll take jobs if there's anything available. They'll go to the cassiterite mines, or try gold mining on the river, or work on the riverboats. Some of them become traders. Others go off to the towns and find work there. They're real survivors. Some of them have moved onto the settlement schemes, and it's fair to say that they've been more successful than the southerners. That's because they understand the forest and the soils a bit better, although I wouldn't say they were good farmers.

I've got a report here done by a team of padres from São Paulo. They call it 'Profile of a River Community.' It says some interesting things. One of the points it makes is how isolated these communities really are. Calama is only ten hours by river from Porto Velho, but there are people living strung out all along the rivers, some of them as much as two days from here by boat. There aren't any roads.

"We have 200 families here, a total of about 1,300 people in all. Somewhere around six and a bit people to a family. It's a homogeneous population; almost all of them come from the area. The only outsiders are a few government people, the five teachers, and a handful of families from further up and down the river.

"It's also a very young community. Nearly two out of three people are under twenty-one. That's a lot of mouths to feed, a lot of children in school. Mind you, it's not a bad school. I've been here a year now. Five of us came from the same town in Ceará to see if we could do something here. We find the town fairly supportive. Most people are more or less literate, surprisingly enough. But there's still a lot of absenteeism in school. I think that it's got something to do with malnutrition. The kids have difficulty keeping up with their work, and they fall behind and have to repeat the year. They feel bad about it, and finally they just give up.

"And they *shouldn't* be malnourished. There's no reason for them not to get the protein they need. There's always plenty of fish. But they tend to eat the wrong things—too much sugar and soft drinks—and manioc isn't really very nourishing. They suffer from a generally low level of health. That's partly because of the malaria and partly because they have a lot of worms and parasites. We're trying to teach them a bit about hygiene, and many of the houses have piped water now; but they still go on drinking water right out of the river.

"Another problem is lack of employment. With no job prospects, they can't see the point of going to school, especially the older kids. They'd rather be playing football. Or making love! That's another thing. They become sexually active very early, and babies get born all over the place. Nobody minds whether a girl has a husband or not. Mostly she doesn't. So a lot of our girls drop out because they get pregnant.

"One good thing. There's no shortage of houses. Almost everyone owns a house of sorts; after all, they're easy to build in these parts. All you need is some kind of roof to keep out the rain.

"They're basically decent people. You must have noticed how friendly they are. Always ready to help out when someone is sick, for example. Look at Dona Morena. Her place is constantly full of waifs and strays. She's wonderful, that woman, and she's by no means the only one.

"But they're a lazy lot. At least I think so! There are things they want, but they're not really prepared to go out and work for them. They're inclined to complain. They want a day nursery for the children, for example. But when I tried to organize a meeting to discuss it, hardly anyone showed up. Then they say they need a few paved roads. Well, that's true. The place turns into a morass in the winter. But they don't seem to have any drive to do a community project to accomplish it. They can all get together on things like supporting the football team, and they all turn up for saints' days and weddings and things like that. But they're not exactly go-getters! I'd say they tend to be pretty passive. Maybe that's the Indian in them. They don't seem to think much about the future and how they could change things. Sometimes I feel they need a good shaking!"

Down on the waterfront we meet a woman who has been in town for a wedding. She is waiting to go upriver in the government boat that is due to sail sometime before nightfall. Small and neat in her faded denim skirt, Dona Maria is happy to talk about life on the river.

"My name is Maria dos Anjos Pereira Silva, and I am forty-six years old," she begins without preamble. "My husband is called Jorge Leal Vianna Pereira, and we have been together for thirty years. We have seven children living, and we lost three. I have eleven grandchildren, and most of the family lives nearby. Our house is about three hours from here, on the Machado River, and my husband is a fisherman. Of course he does a bit of hunting as well, but there isn't much game left in those parts. I remember when I was a girl we could always get a nice bit of peccary, but it isn't so easy these days.

"Where was I? Oh yes, my husband. He catches fish and salts them. He sells them when he can. My job is looking after the house and the fields and the livestock, of course. I've got one boy at home to help me with the heavy work, and my eldest, he goes out with Jorge. Then there's two girls with us; Maria is nineteen—a fine baby she's got—and Luciana, although I don't think she'll be around for long, not with her looks. The eldest boy, he's got it into his head to go off and be a gold miner next year; he says he can make a much better living that way. That's true enough, although I can't say I'm happy about his decision. A rough lot those gold miners are, and you're always hearing stories of them getting into fights and getting themselves shot. My Jorge, he went off there once, just to take a look. Came right back, he did. Didn't want to live on one of those dredgers, he said, with all that mud, and so much noise you can't hear yourself think. He'd rather stick to his fishing. And as for all those gunfights . . . I don't want João to get mixed up in that sort of thing. He's a good boy.

"Every second Saturday we come up to town. I have a little stall in the market. I sell medicines—roots and leaves for making teas and lotions. I've always been interested in such things. My mother taught me a lot about them when I was a girl, and most of the people around here ask me to help them out when they're sick. My youngest girl, she comes in with us, and she helps me out on the stall. We usually do quite well on market day, and we come back with enough to keep us going. Not that we buy much, you understand, but salt, cooking oil, perhaps a length of cloth, kerosene for the lamps, ammunition, that sort of thing.

"We don't have to buy any food, of course. We plant manioc, corn, rice, and beans. We've got some fruit trees: papaya, oranges, cupuaçu, and bananas. We keep chickens, and there's no shortage of fish! We never go hungry, I can tell you. Not like those people who live in Porto Velho. My second girl, she must be twenty-five or twenty-six now. Well, she went off to live in the city. Her husband said *he* wasn't going to spend his life working like a donkey in the forest. He wanted electricity, running water, a bar to go to in the evenings, television, that sort of thing. So what does he do? Last I heard he was working in a warehouse, carrying boxes back and forth all day. If that isn't working like a donkey, I don't know what is.

"And they live in this *tiny* little house. Electricity? Oh yes, they've got that. One of his friends wired their house into the mains—they all do that there—and they've got their television all right. Running water? *Nada!* There's a tap at the end of the street, but half the time it's dry and they have to get the water from the river. If the cholera arrives there, I don't know what will happen to them.

"She goes out to work too, my daughter does. They can't live on what he earns—not in a town. Why, you have to buy everything. You can't just go out back and pick it out of the garden. She's only got the one baby—just as well, I say—and so she leaves it with a neighbor and works in a butcher's shop—cleans the place and makes the coffee. I can't see the fun of that, I must say, all that blood all over the place! Still, it's close to home, and she can pop in and see how the baby's doing. Not that it seems to do very well, poor little thing. It's always getting sick. I send her some of my herbs and roots when I can, but I don't believe she uses them. 'Oh no, mother,' she says. 'I'll get him something from the pharmacy.' Only she usually can't afford to buy stuff from there, and half the time it's no good anyway, if you ask me.

"There are a lot of people who think that they'll get better only if they have an injection. So they take themselves off to the pharmacist, and he sticks a needle in their arm and charges them 500 cruzeiros [nearly a day's salary], and they figure they're cured. It can't be good for them, all these needles they keep putting into themselves. They'd be far better off using my remedies. Well, *they* may look down on them, but there's plenty who don't, and many's the person that I've cured from the fever, or ulcers, or difficult childbirth. Still, God be praised, I have a good family. All nice children, although you do worry sometimes, don't you? And I have all my grandchildren, and my health, and a good man, if I do say so myself.

"Problems? Oh, yes! Who hasn't? We're a long way from the town, for instance. It takes us three or four hours upriver. It'd be nice if we had a better engine for the canoe. We used to have a good one, but we had to sell it a year or two back. No, I don't mind not having the electricity. It's what you're used to, you see. But I would like to be nearer a school. None of my children had the chance to go, but I think *their* children ought to have the opportunity. And it would be nice if we had a better health post. The malaria is bad down our way. And there's another thing. I like to hear Mass every once in a while. Sometimes we stay on in Calama after market, but not often. We usually have to get back. I like it on the river, you see. I don't like to be away."

Dona Maria gathers her bundles and goes off down the steps to board the boat. We wander off along the riverbank and sit down to watch the dolphins.

In the cool early evening, we make our way out of the village through a field of manioc and into the forest. In a small clearing we come across a fisherman called Sebastião. His tiny house on stilts overlooks a magnificent sweep of river. Next to the house is an identical smaller structure for the hens. It is decorated with chickens' wings.

Sebastião's wife left him some time ago; she now lives with her daughter at the other end of the village. One of his granddaughters comes and cooks for him and takes care of his clothes. Since his accident—he slipped and ran the point of his machete into his chest, narrowly missing his heart—he doesn't have the strength he did and can't work much. He spends a lot of time sitting on a bench he has built under a large shady tree, looking out over the river.

"Well, I can't get about as much as I used to, more's the pity," he begins. "But I can still catch the odd fish, and I have the chickens and a bit of manioc that one of my sons helps me with. He sometimes brings me something for the pot when he goes hunting; although there's a lot of jaguars about, and it's not so safe anymore.

"Very tricky animals, jaguars, as I expect you know. They'll sneak up on you from behind. I think they're bolder these days when it comes to attacking people. I don't know why that should be. But there was one that finished off old José not three months back, and they found it had been following him for miles before it got him. He didn't have any bullets left. I don't know whether he had a shot at it or not.

"I never did like that patch of forest. They say that's where the Mapinguari walks. I haven't seen it myself, but I had an uncle who did, and he said it fair froze the blood in your bones. It's all hairy, with one eye in the middle of its forehead—looks like a big monkey and cries like a child. And it has a dreadful smell. They say that if you are hiding up a tree and it stands underneath, the smell is enough to make you sick.

"The Great Snake, on the other hand, I've seen *that* often enough. Do you see that sandbank over there? Well, there's a snake that lives in the mouth of that creek just behind. He hides up there and catches the small fish as they swim in and out. Sometimes you can see him swimming across the river at night. He has his head right out of the water, and a queer light shines out of his eyes. He makes a noise like the sound of an engine. They say he pulls people out of their canoes and takes them down to the bottom of the river."

The river people, like the Indians, have worse things to fear than the Mapinguari and the Great Snake. All Amazônians are threatened by poverty, by disease, and by the influx of newcomers to the region. Unlike the Indians, the *caboclos* have one grave disadvantage: Like poor, unpicturesque peasants everywhere, they are not newsworthy. They do not have pop singers and human-rights activists fighting for them, as the Indians do. They are the forgotten people of the Amazon.

But they are also survivors. They are not to be pushed around so easily. The *caboclos*, although frequently subjected to long cycles of exploitation, are less docile than their masters would hope. A doughty people, they have a history of revolt dating from the great Cabanagem rebellion in the 1830s, when they stormed the prison in Belém, murdered the president of Pará, and started a decade-long uprising that spread up the river all the way to the Peruvian border.

From time to time, different governments have fondly hoped that they could turn Amazônia into the breadbasket of Brazil. But the rebellious inhabitants of the area preferred to live by their wits—collecting rubber and nuts from the forest, hunting, fishing, and growing their own food. From the early days, the *caboclos*, poor as they were, lived with a certain degree of autonomy. They were slaves to no man.

The area in which the river people live is the subject of intense debate locally and worldwide. Yet they do not see the issues being discussed as the most important ones. What most concerns them is day-to-day survival. We asked Dona Morena and her husband, Pedro, what they felt were their greatest needs.

Pedro is a dashing figure, given to wearing tight jeans with a gold chain on his bare chest. He owns a couple of pieces of land, a riverboat, and the biggest food store in town. He has plenty of ideas about the future of Calama, and his plans include becoming the mayor—if the place ever becomes a city.

"Well, I suppose the main problem, and that's true throughout Rondônia, is the pressure on the land. It didn't used to be a problem; there was room for everyone and you could always find a place to grow your crops. But it's different now. It's all these new people coming in—the settlers and miners, and the loggers, and the ranchers, of course. Just too many people! It leads to overfishing and a shortage of game. And worse.

"There are a lot of changes in the river itself too, partly because of all the forest being cut. The whole pattern of flooding is changing, and since we grow most of our food on the floodplains, that's serious—although I don't think many people realize it yet. The culprits are the gold miners. All that drilling in the riverbed is altering the navigation channels, and the mercury they use is poisoning the water and killing off the fish. There's places where you catch a fish and open it up and it's all rotten inside.

"We're very isolated here too. The world we see on television, for example, could be a million miles away. Television does keep us in touch, to a certain extent, but what it shows us is how very backward we are!"

"Not as backward as the people out in the colonies," puts in Dona Morena. "They can't even get the television out there. They have to get their news from the radio—that and the riverboats. It's a hard life for them. There's so much malaria, for one thing. If they don't treat it properly they get hepatitis, and that's the killer. The children are always full of worms, and that weakens them, so they're susceptible to flu and pneumonia.

"When they are sick, this is the nearest place for them to come. Not that there's much here—only a small health clinic and precious little equipment. They haven't sent us any drugs for five weeks now.

"I suppose the worst thing for the settlers is the lack of transport. You can't rely on the government boat. It's supposed to go twice a month, but that's only if there's money for fuel. So you can never tell when it's going to go. It was here this week, but that was the first time for nearly a month.

"I think that because we live so far from the city, the government forgets about us. They're just not interested. Except at election time, then they promise us the moon. But they never deliver anything!"

"Well," said Pedro, "things *are* improving. Although you can't expect too much with the economic situation the way it is. There's been a noticeable increase in river traffic, for example, since the road to Manaus has been closed. That's got to be good for the river communities. Although some of them are still very isolated. Those settlement schemes that Morena was talking about, they're two days upriver from here. The government boat is supposed to go up there, but it never does. Even when you do get there, you still have to travel another fifteen miles inland. They have a tractor that meets the boat, but half the time it's broken down, and nobody's got the money to fix it. So you can imagine what it's like for those people trying to sell their produce. There was talk of putting in a road to link with the BR-364, but it seems there's a cassiterite mining company there that won't allow the road to go through. They say it belongs to the Queen of England.

"Of course a lot of people want to move to the city. Most families have some relative or other in town, so they've got a roof over their heads if they need to see a doctor, or if they want to look for a job. Some families even send a child or two to high school.

"Those that do move to the city don't have an easy time of it, let me tell you. It's hard to get jobs, and they have to rely on friends and family until they get going. And living conditions aren't easy. In fact I'd say that most people live better in the country. It's more healthy, except for the areas where the malaria is bad. But the younger people seem to want the facilities of a town, and I don't know that you can blame them. Families aren't sticking together like they used to."

"Well, I can tell you one thing," continued Morena. "If this place ever becomes a city, we've got a long list of things we want. We need a preschool for the children. We want a padre—there hasn't been one in Calama for three years now, and the evangelical churches are stealing all our people away. We want to upgrade the market. It's ridiculous that we have to rely so much on tinned goods. We'd like to make a better landing stage. You've seen how difficult it is getting heavy stuff up that riverbank.

"We really need a dentist, too. And a better system of dealing with people who have to get to the hospital in a hurry. A big speedboat would be the thing. At the moment we just see whose canoe we can borrow, and that's not very satisfactory.

"We want to pave the roads. In the rains, this place is a nightmare to walk about in, with mud all over. And we really ought to do something about the drains.

"So you see, Pedro, when you get to be mayor, there'll be plenty for you to do!"

6

MINERS

Were't not for gold and women, there would be no damnation.

—Cyril Tourneur, 1620

"You want to know about gold mining, you've come to the right person." Lincoln plunked himself down on the sofa and lit the first of what seemed like a million cigarettes. "I've been in the business for ten years, chasing gold all over Brazil, one end of the country to the other. I'll take you out on the river any time you like and you can see for yourself. It's a tough life, but after a bit it gets to you. I've never hit the really big time, although I've done all right. But it won't let you go, you know. Every time you think, well, I've just about had enough of this, something tells you there's a lucky streak just around the corner.

"I'll tell you a bit about it first, because once you get on that dredger, it's kind of hard to talk. Too much going on, and the machinery makes a hell of a racket.

"First of all, there's three different types of operations on the river here. The most primitive is the barge, which has the drilling equipment mounted underneath. It's handled by a diver, and it's a very risky business. He doesn't have oxygen tanks, he uses an air pipe. Those things can easily get caught up in the drilling equipment or in some floating debris, and that's it for the diver. They work continuously, twenty-four hours a day, but of course they can't do it when the water's above about sixty-five feet, or when it's too turbulent. A lot of them take drugs, and there's a lot of accidents. Divers don't last long around these parts."

45

We were extraordinarily lucky to have made friends with Lincoln when we got to Porto Velho, Rondônia. Everyone had told us that it was too dangerous for two women to visit the *garimpo* where the gold miners worked. We probably wouldn't even be able to find anyone willing to talk to us, said the local experts, since almost everything about the *garimpo* is illegal. But we persisted, and our luck turned when we met Lincoln. He couldn't tell us enough about his favorite topic: gold.

"There are two types of dredger," he continued, lighting up again. "We call them *dragas.* One has a fixed probe mounted in front. You can move the probe up and down, but not from side to side. They're suitable for deep dredging, so we're not using them now. The water's too low. The ones we're using have probes mounted underneath, and you can move them sideways as well as up and down. Gives you a lot more flexibility.

"I'll show you the whole process tomorrow. My brother and I have got four *dragas* working down by the rapids at Teotonio. OK if I meet you downstairs at seven?" He uncoiled himself from his seat and adjusted a strand of hair behind one ear. "Bring your camera if you want to take some shots."

The next morning at seven o'clock we climbed up into Lincoln's big truck, together with two burly long-haired men and several packs of cigarettes. First stop was to collect a spare part. "Won't take a second," said Lincoln cheerfully. "They radioed last night and told me what they needed."

He swung the truck around into a side street full of workshops supplying parts for the dredgers. A fleet of taxis stood outside the biggest one, and a procession of tough-looking men emerged with steel cables, drill bits, and all manner of spares. "We can always get what we need. Twenty-four hours a day, 365 days a year. We can't afford to stop drilling, so we've got to have access to parts." Lincoln vanished into the depths of the shop and didn't emerge for nearly an hour. We sat sweatily outside, listening to deafening tapes of Elton John.

"Sorry to keep you." He emerged cheerily, heaving a long length of cable into the back. "We'll just pick up something for lunch, and then we're on our way."

He headed off west along the BR-364. About twenty miles later, a dirt road branched off to the waterfall at Teotonio. "The pools below waterfalls and at the bottom of rapids are great places for gold," Lincoln explained. "The gold dust seems to collect there."

The river appeared, along with a little settlement of wooden buildings housing bars, repair shops, and eating places. It's a favorite spot for Sunday picnics—a pleasantly quiet pool below the foaming waterfall.

Lincoln's canoe was waiting at the water's edge, and we piled aboard with the spare parts, shot a small rapid, and pulled out into the main river. The water was utterly still and mirror calm, and it was glaringly hot on the river.

We rounded the corner and saw the first *dragas,* clumsy barges on floats like barrage balloons; they looked distinctly homemade. Roughly carpentered platforms about eleven yards in length held all the drilling equipment, and a cabin built above one end housed the living quarters. Hammocks were swinging above the machinery. Space was at a premium. Reaching out from the front was a long rusty probe with a spiky head called an *abacaxi*—which translates as "pineapple" and describes it perfectly. The atmosphere was one of stern attention to duty. Everybody was hard at work. The men scarcely looked up from tending the noisy machinery as we passed, and the occasional woman in tight shorts and cutoff top looked at us incuriously through a haze of cigarette smoke.

The *dragas* huddle together in groups, constantly jockeying for position and nosing one another out of the way, not always in a gentle manner. Since the *dragas* have no means of propulsion, motorboats are used to shift them around, and the kaleidoscope of *dragas* is continually moving and reforming itself.

"There's times when some guy will sneak up and cut your anchor cable in order to get on your gold," said Lincoln. "Back in '88, when they were hauling gold out by the bucketful, sometimes you'd have to wave a machine gun under their noses before they'd back off. But it's not so bad these days. Far fewer people on the river for one thing. There isn't nearly the gold there used to be. So things have settled down a bit. Come aboard."

We stepped across the cluttered deck. The noise was deafening. The engineer was sitting on an old car seat. Like everyone else, he wore greasy shorts and flip-flops. He was in charge of the drilling and in constant touch with another crew hand who was testing the inflow of water for gold dust, to see whether they were on target.

"The riverbed has got layers of sand and shingle on top, and then gravel and clay," explained Lincoln. "We've got to find out where the gold is and stay at that depth. The material we're drilling is mostly pebbles and sand, although sometimes we get some bigger rocks. It all gets pumped up that big pipe there and sprayed out into the top tank. Then it passes through a sort of sieve that catches the larger pebbles and rocks, and runs down a slope that is covered with carpet and ridged with little wooden baffles to catch the gold dust. Gold is heavier than sand, so it tends to get caught, and the running water carries the sand off."

We gazed, mesmerized, at the constant flow of water running down the carpeted surface. A crew member stood underneath the outflow, collecting material in a shallow pan and scrutinizing it for signs of gold dust. Sometimes the water would flow dark red, sometimes deep gray, sometimes almost green. "That's the different layers of the riverbed," explained Lincoln.

"The next stage is the concentration. The baffles are removed, the carpets are brushed down and shaken, and the mixture of sand and gold dust is hosed off into a large barrel and mixed with mercury. It takes roughly 2 pounds of mercury to amalgamate 1 pound of gold. We use a large rotary beater, like a giant eggbeater, and after twenty minutes or so we're left with a little ball of mercury and gold.

"After that we do the refining. Come upstairs and I'll show you." He led the way up creaking steps to a little galley at the top. The cook had placed pans full of rice, spaghetti, beans, and meat sauce on the table. There was the inevitable thermos of hot, sweet coffee and bottles of cloudy water from the freezer. Lincoln caught us exchanging glances and laughed. "The water's OK. We get it from the creek. But I think there's some soda, if you'd rather." We accepted sodas wordlessly.

Now came the tricky part. The toxic mixture of gold and mercury had to be separated. The process usually takes place near the kitchen, to take advantage of the cook's gas cylinder. The fact that the mercury fumes are in an excellent position to contaminate all the food appeared to pass unnoticed. Lincoln swore that he recycled his mercury. At the price he paid for it, he couldn't afford to waste it. He told us that the still was airtight. He said that if any mercury did fall into the river—which of course it wouldn't, and certainly not off his *draga*—it would sink to the bottom and not harm anyone. It would be impossible for the fish to eat it, because it would settle on the riverbed, below the weeds they browse in. The concept of the weeds taking up the mercury seemed to be a new one to him.

We held our breath.

One of the crew squatted over the gas cylinder, cigarette dangling between his lips, and connected it to the burner. He then applied a blowtorch to the mixture. As the mercury burnt off, it was distilled and the gold dust was revealed—on this occasion about a tablespoonful.

The gold was then ceremoniously taken in to be weighed—an event attended by everyone. It is divided up eighty percent to the owner (who in this case is also the manager) and twenty percent to the workers. The owner is responsible for operating and maintenance costs as well as all expenses for food and transport. The cook gets paid about half an ounce of gold a month, and if she does the washing for the crew, each of them pays her 0.07 ounces a month. Gold dust is the common currency used by everyone in the *garimpo:* Wages are paid in it, supplies are purchased in it, and cash is scarcely used at all.

We chatted with the crew. They were all friendly and relaxed; there had been a reasonable amount of gold, and everyone was in a good mood. One old man told that us he had been a miner on and off for years. He had worked all over Amazônia—down in the south, over in Serra Pelada. "But I like the river best," he said. "And we've got a good bunch here." Another crew member was a former air steward from VARIG (the largest Brazilian airline). He spoke some English and managed to be immaculate in neatly pressed shorts.

There was not the smallest regard for safety—nothing to stop you falling off the edge or catching a toe or a finger in the machinery. At one stage a neighboring *draga* got the edge of its float caught up on ours, and several men spent some time ineffectually attempting to lever it off. Finally their companions came along, leaned their backs against the side of our *draga*, and pushed with their feet. Protestingly, the two *dragas* came apart, and bare toes curled out of the way of disaster.

"How do you know where the gold is?" I asked Lincoln.

"We don't," he answered. "There *are* maps, but we don't have access to them. But you get the feel for it. Working by the seat of your pants. The gold often runs in veins across the river, and on river bends it gets deposited on the inside of the downstream curve. The bank on a curve is usually a great place to drill.

"I'm very superstitious. We all are. If I see a butterfly, or a certain type of bird, I'll know there's gold there. I don't know *how* I know, I just seem to. There's other guys that reckon they can find gold by numbers, or cards, or even magic. Of course it's quite hard to orient yourself on the river. I usually eyeball it from some landmark on the shore, a tree or something, and then I drop the anchor and just concentrate on keeping on top of that gold.

"If you *are* on the gold, you won't be the only one. The others will be on you like a swarm of locusts! But in this part of the river there's a good feeling among the *dragas*. These days, anyway. There's an unwritten law, for example, that anyone can board anyone else's *draga*, sleep if he feels like it, eat if he wants to. We help each other out with spare parts when we can, and that sort of thing. And we borrow each other's motorboats to move our *dragas* around.

"But that doesn't mean there isn't a lot of poaching and general carrying on. And you have to have strict rules. I never allow any liquor on my *dragas*. Nor women. And I don't let the guys use cocaine when they're on the job. Not that I object to cocaine. It's no worse than anything else, as far as I know, and addicts make good workers. They need to work, and they work like demons. I let the boys go off home every once in a while, and I always say to them, 'Boys, you can screw around and get smashed all you want. But not on my *draga*, OK?' And they respect that."

Ever since the days of the conquistadors, people have searched for El Dorado all over the Amazon. Pizarro and his men found nothing, but they didn't look under the forest floor.

What lies there has value beyond imagining. It is enough to transform Brazil into one of the most powerful countries in the world. The respected Brazilian geologist João Orestes Schneider dos Santos points out that the mineral resources of Amazônia are sufficient not only to pay off the external debt of $120 billion, *but also to finance the U.S. national debt of more than a trillion dollars.*

It's hard to obtain accurate figures for mineral resources in Amazônia. I take mine from a 1989 article in *Veja* magazine, a reliable source. The article asserts that the Amazon can provide substantial amounts of aluminum, copper, tin, tungsten, manganese, uranium, iron, gold, diamonds, nickel, potassium, niobium, limestone, natural gas, and petroleum. Take a look at the figures:

- *Aluminum:* Nhamunda, Amazonas. Reserves valued at $1.1 billion. Large deposits also in Trombetas and Cachoeira Porteira in Pará.

- *Tin:* Presidente Figueiredo, Amazonas. Valued at $2.8 billion. Also nearby at Pitinga and Balbina.

- *Iron:* From Carajás alone, valued at nearly $500 million a year. There are still untouched reserves of zinc, lead, cobalt, molybdenum, tungsten, and tantalum. Gold, copper, manganese, nickel, and bauxite are also being exploited.

- *Potassium:* Nova Olinda do Norte, Amazonas. Reserves valued at $24 million.

- *Niobium:* São Gabriel do Cachoeira, Amazonas, has seventy-eight percent of the known resources in the world. Valued at $28 billion.

- *Lime:* Nhamunda, Amazonas. Valued at $500 million.

- *Natural gas:* Tefé, Amazonas. Valued at $15.5 billion.

- *Gold:* Rio Maués, Amazonas. Valued at $800 million. There are other deposits on the Tapajós; at Carajás, Trombetas, and Serra Pelada in Pará, in Amapá, in Roraima, and on the Madeira River.

The income from these resources already exceeds $3.5 billion a year.

How is Brazil exploiting this unparalleled bonanza? First, by granting concessions to big national and multinational mining companies. Second, by permitting, if not actually encouraging, the activities of large numbers of independent miners, known as *garimpeiros.*

There is considerable friction between the two camps. The mining companies maintain that their methods are far more efficient than the ones used by the *garimpeiros* and that they provide better and safer conditions, as well as more money at the end of the day. They point out that they contribute far more to the state in the form of both infrastructure and income.

The mining companies also cause considerable environmental damage. Large amounts of human waste and mercury run off into the rivers. During the wet season, the mining sites turn into seas of mud that provide ideal conditions for the breeding of malarial mosquitoes.

As for the independent miners, they participate in the largest business in the Amazon. Gold mining involves, at one time or another, probably half a million men—approximately a third of the working population of the region. In terms of production, it is second only to the mining of iron ore.

Although the government may not like the idea, it is advantageous to permit the *garimpeiros* to operate; the *garimpo* provides a livelihood for large numbers of otherwise unemployed workers. *Garimpeiros* have a keen nose for locating gold, but they are highly mobile and extremely hard to control. Most of their gold goes undeclared and therefore untaxed. In fact, most things to do with the *garimpo* are clandestine. Few of the *dragas* are registered, their radios operate on illegal frequencies, most of the men have no identity papers, and many of them use false names. The *garimpo* generates considerable pollution in terms of human waste, diesel fuel, and poisonous mercury. It is also a focus for disease, drugs, drinking, prostitution, murder and mayhem.

The *garimpeiros* frequently invade Indian areas in pursuit of gold. Their presence is a mixed blessing for the Indians. On the one hand, they provide cash that can pay for demarcation of territory, planes, trucks, medical care, and a measure of financial independence from the feeble embrace of FUNAI. On the other hand, they cheat the Indians, introduce drugs and alcohol, and bring white man's diseases to which the Indians have no immunity. The use of mercury poses an especially subtle and serious health risk.

To understand the seeming abandon with which the *garimpeiros* are contaminating themselves and everybody else with mercury, it may be helpful to know just who they are. They are young men, most of them between the ages of fifteen and twenty-five. They come to the *garimpo* because it is their best option. Some come from distant parts of the country, but many are local *caboclos*. They move in and out of the *garimpo* as necessity and weather dictate, alternating stints on the *garimpo* with working on farms, or rubber tapping, or being messengers and general drudges in the towns. Their living conditions are precarious, and their life expectancy is short, not least because of the mercury.

Mercury can be poisonous in several ways. It can be absorbed through the skin. It can be ingested when mercury-laden dust lands on food or utensils or by eating contaminated fish. Even very small amounts can cause chronic poisoning, since mercury penetrates the nervous system, where it accumulates. Symptoms of mercury poisoning include irritability, difficulty in hearing, kidney problems, insomnia, low fever, manic-depressive behavior, loss of memory, birth defects, and madness.

On all counts, the *garimpeiro* is doing considerable damage to himself, to his environment, and to the people nearby. Most of the gold he produces will bypass the coffers of the government. Yet there's something of the free-spirited, picaresque hero about the *garimpeiro* that appeals to every romantic soul. Even if he could be controlled, why should he not be allowed his chance?

Back in town we talked to Marlene, the wife of a *garimpeiro* who is currently working on the Madeira River in Bolivia. Marlene is a comfortable brunette with a big heart.

"Ludwig isn't here now, but I'll tell you a bit about it if you like. We've been here for about, oh, six months I suppose. We've got several *dragas* on the Madeira River.

"Ludwig used to work right here, near the city, but then the mayor decided to stop the *garimpeiros* from working here. He said the *dragas* were interfering with the navigation channels. So they sent in the navy, and they untied the *dragas* and let them drift over the rapids. Ludwig stationed a man just below to catch ours, but he missed one of them as it came over, and it sank. It's there now till the water goes down.

"So Ludwig's working in Bolivia just now. The police there aren't so strict. And what a job it is. They're very rough, the *garimpeiros*, you know. Ludwig won't let me go anywhere near the *draga.* Says it's much too dangerous for a woman. You should *see* him when he comes home. *Covered* in mud! He always says he doesn't feel really clean till he's had at least two showers, and I have a terrible job with his clothes.

"The things that go on at the *garimpo,* you wouldn't believe. Last time he was back he told a hair-raising story of bodies floating down the river. There's plenty of violence and fighting, you know. Ludwig won't let anybody take liquor on board when he's there, but the other *garimpeiros* do, of course, and there's always fights and people getting knifed and shot. Well, it seems that this body came floating down the river, and one of the fellows said to Ludwig 'Look! There's a gold watch on that body. I'll have that.' So he went and got a boat hook and pulled the body in, but it was all swollen up and he couldn't get the watch off. He yelled to the cook, 'Cookie! Let's have that knife of yours over here.' So the cook sent it over to him, and he cut off the arm, and finally managed to get the watch. He went to show it to the cook, and she said, 'Where did you get that?' And he said, 'I just cut it off a body floating down the river.' And the cook said, 'Well, that's the last time I lend you a knife of mine then!'

"The *dragas* usually operate together in groups of nine or ten. Are you familiar with the word *fofoca*? It means gossip. They call them *fofocas,* because they look like a collection of old ladies gossiping. They rope the *dragas* together and they all work in the same place. If anyone needs a push, there's always a motorboat somewhere around. There's lots of other barges around the place—bars, drugstores, repairmen, barbers, brothels, water taxis, and all sorts of little traders selling just about everything. There's no need for the men to come off the *dragas* at all. Everything is right there at hand. Next time Ludwig comes back you ought to talk to him. He'll have lots to tell you."

Ludwig hit town the very next day. He swept into the apartment like a hurricane and settled himself uncomfortably on the white sofa. He looked out of place in Marlene's delicately feminine sitting room.

I asked him about the future of the *garimpo.*

"You want to know what I think? Well, I think it's pretty damned limited, that's what I think. It won't be long before we're out of here. Already the place is only a shadow of what it was. If you'd have been here two or three years back, the river would have been so full of *dragas* you couldn't hardly see any water! But that's all changed. For a start, the gold is coming deeper these days. That means that our equipment can't really touch it. And to get the sort of rig I need is going to cost me *big* bucks—one million of them, to be exact! And do you think anyone in his right mind is going to commit that sort of money with the economic situation the way it is at present? It's only the mining companies that can make that sort of investment.

"I've got 240,000 acres of land up in Amazonas—mineral rights and all—and a whole lot of machinery in Manaus, rusting away. I can't afford to open the place up. That's pretty stupid isn't it?

"And do you know what? I figure I'm getting too old for this game. It isn't the fun it used to be. Back in the old days the place was really humming. Why, even the police didn't dare come into the *garimpo*. It was all liquor and guns, and bodies all over the place. Man, it would get wild! Mind you, I still carry a machine gun when I'm going in and out of the *garimpo*. You never know when some little jerk is going to take it into his head to try to stick you up when you've got the gold in your pocket.

"The *dragas* now, they'll run you $200,000 apiece, easy. As for repairs, it's a bottomless pit! I had to replace all the roofs last week because of some damned storm or other. Just peeled them off like opening cans of sardines.

"I figure each *draga* can produce about ten pounds of gold a month. Depends on all sorts of things, of course. I've got to be on top of the men, for a start. Funny how they never make much gold when I'm not around. And you have to have the best equipment you can afford, and keep it in really good shape. There's other variables too. Like the depth of the water, which isn't predictable from one year to the next, and the different levels of concentration of the gold. I figure it costs me a good thirty percent of the takings to keep the thing running. Some say it's a bit less, but don't you believe them! And eighty percent of my costs goes for maintenance and repairs. Of course the suppliers charge us a fortune. Everyone connected with this business preys on us like a bunch of leeches. They charge us two or three times the going price for every damn thing: parts, food, services, you name it.

"Where do I sell the gold? Well, I'm not about to tell you all my secrets! Sometimes I'll sell it in Porto Velho. Of course I use a lot right here. I'm sure you know that everything to do with the *garimpo* is payable in gold. Sometimes I'll sell it in São Paulo, because there's a better price down there, or Bolivia—no receipts asked or given. Some of the guys get themselves mixed up in diamond trading or cocaine. But the *garimpeiros* won't end up with lots of cash. They'll spend their gold on women and liquor and trying to recover their health.

"This business plays havoc with your health. I must have had malaria twelve or thirteen times. And it doesn't do the liver any good. I can hardly drink anymore. And I've had to give up smoking too. You can see the gut I've got on me. [He pats his huge girth ruefully.] So damn fat I can't fit into any of my clothes. There's precious little fun left around here, now I come to think of it. They say there's enough gold in these rivers to last another thirty years. But I won't be around that long. Not the way I'm living. That mercury isn't doing me any good either. People will tell you they're not poisoning themselves. Balls! The stuff is lethal. Maybe if they put the price way up, then more of them would care about recycling it. At the moment they're just chucking it into the river like there's no tomorrow. And if you're interested in that ecological stuff you might care to think about all the fuel that's going into the river too. To say nothing of human waste and good old-fashioned garbage.

"You'll hear a lot about conditions on the *garimpo*—drinking and drugs, women and murder. It's all true. Most guys don't expect to be on the *garimpo* for very long. They all hope they can make their pile and get out while the going is good. Doesn't happen that way, most of the time. It's a hard life: grinding work night and day, stinking heat, noise, diesel fumes. And for what? For that big strike that's always just around the corner.

"But we've had good times. Trouble is, the damned government can never make up its mind whether it's going to support us or not. I mean, the *garimpo* performs a social service, if you know what I mean. To start with, it keeps a whole lot of boys out of trouble. And it spins off plenty of service industries: the guys who make the *dragas*, the repairmen, the people who supply spare parts and fuel and all kinds of stuff, including booze and women—even those sharks that buy the gold.

"Every so often we get closed down. They send the navy in to move us along, and that can lead to some pretty ugly scenes, let me tell you! But then those idiots in Brasília can't bring themselves to encourage the big companies either. I mean, strictly speaking, they should be supporting them up to the hilt. They provide stable employment and much better conditions for their workers, and they sure as hell declare a lot more of their revenue! But the state just pussyfoots around and lets the *garimpeiros* go swarming about. The companies get robbed right and left, often by their own employees, but when they try to set up some sort of effective security system, the press says that they're employing a bunch of thugs, and sometimes they decide it just isn't worth the effort. It's too bad, because half the time they can't even get any workers. The guys all want to be on the *garimpo!* As for the *garimpeiros*, all they're doing is throwing their money away, ruining their health, and poisoning the rivers. So it's a kind of Catch-22 situation. And that's absurd, because this place has got more natural resources than anywhere else in the whole damned world.

"Sometimes I say to myself, 'What the hell are you doing in this damned country anyway?' And you know what? Sometimes I'm damned if I know!"

7

SETTLERS

This is what I prayed for; a plot of land and a bit of forest.

—Horace, 65 B.C.

Suppose a government faces two problems: millions of its people are landless and destitute, and there are vast areas of land that need to be opened up for development. What could be more logical than to bring the people to the land? The people would need access, support until they got going, and some infrastructure, but the empty spaces would be populated and the empty bellies satisfied. Hard-working peasants could grow abundant food to feed millions of urban poor.

For the last thirty years, the government of Brazil has made vigorous efforts to fit the two parts of the equation together by moving the people without land to the land without people. For many reasons, these attempts have met with mixed results.

Nobody had any experience running settlement schemes, which are far more complex in reality than they are on paper. For instance, look at what happened in 1967 when the road from Brasília to Belém was built. Instead of facilitating the settlement of landless peasants, to the mutual advantage of both state and peasant, it led to wholesale deforestation. Reasonable laws weren't in place—and nobody respected them anyway. Then the land grabbers snatched the land, and before anybody realized what was happening, the peasants had been kicked out and replaced by many large unprofitable ranches. The results, in terms of ruined land and widespread violence, linger to this day.

The National Integration Program of 1970 was designed to open up Amazônia by building a magnificent new highway across it. Landless northeasterners were to be lured there with construction jobs on the Transamazônica and settled on the land. But the northeasterners were reluctant to come and didn't like it when they did. Accustomed to harsh, dry conditions, they found themselves in harsh, wet conditions. The soils, which everyone had assumed were lush and fertile, turned out to be unexpectedly weak. The settlers didn't manage to grow many crops, and what they did grow they couldn't market. Malaria was rife, attacking most strongly at harvesttime. This meant that many settlers couldn't harvest, and those that could encountered problems with transport. The road wasn't a big success. It cost a lot, but it was built in such a hurry that no one considered that underneath all those trees were bits that were higher, bits that were lower, and bits that were much too wet to build a workable road on at all.

Some of the settlers did all right—mostly those who ignored government advice to grow rice, corn, and beans and instead diversified into manioc, peanuts, tobacco, poultry, and pigs. Those whose families could provide a wage earner fared reasonably well. Labor is always scarce on the frontier, and wages are high. Still others prospered by mining gold.

The next big government scheme, Polonoroeste, was located in Rondônia. We talked to one of the government officials who had been involved with Polonoroeste from its beginnings in the early 1980s. Carlos Leonardo lives in Cacoal, Rondônia, and he works for the State Forestry Institute now. He has a small farm nearby and is passionately interested in trying out new systems of mixed crops. He is the husband of Maria *dos indios*—the one who took us to visit the Suruí.

"We must be among the earliest arrivals in this part of the world," he told us. "Maria and I came up more than twenty years ago. There wasn't a tarmac road in those days. It was quite an adventure; it used to take two weeks or longer from Cuiabá. Now it's just about twenty hours.

"We'd both always wanted to go to Amazônia. I'm from Rio Grande; Maria is from Minas. When we heard that Rondônia was opening up to settlement, we thought we must get in on it. After all, it's history in the making.

"In the beginning the only people living in this area were the Indians and the river people—*ribeirinhos* we call them. They lived by doing a little hunting, a little fishing, and maybe a bit of rubber tapping. They grew a few crops on the riverbanks, just like they do nowadays: beans and manioc and sometimes rice or corn.

"Nobody else came here much. There weren't any roads, and the whole place was under forest. The only way to travel was by river. There was some traffic on the Madeira River, but only as far as Porto Velho. You can't go any higher because of the rapids. Well, in 1912 they put in the railroad, and after that the telegraph line. Then in 1960 they started work on the BR-364.

"The military government wanted to occupy Amazônia, so they started the settlement schemes, first in Pará and then on the Transamazônica. They had inherited former President Vargas' idea of Greater Brazil; they were afraid that if they didn't occupy the Amazon somebody else would! General Golbery [the chief of National Security] used to talk about 'flooding the place with civilization.' And they were worried that people over in the northeast might foment a revolution, since things were so bad over there.

"But they didn't have much luck with those early settlements, so they decided to organize things a bit better in Rondônia. They had to, because this was to be the biggest scheme yet, with most of the money coming from the World Bank. Polonoroeste was to be a magnet for development in the northwest, and the idea was to create a climate for voluntary settlement—not like the Transamazônica, where they'd actually put people in planes and flown them in. Here in Rondônia, the government reckoned that if it created the right conditions, settlers would bring themselves. Well, it was more successful than anyone dreamed. People came flooding in. You'd have thought they were after gold, not just a piece of land!

"Most of them came from the south: Paraná, Minas, São Paulo. They'd started mechanizing the farms down there, and all the small farmers were driven out. I believe it was something like seventeen million people in all who got pushed off the land. Most of them ended up in the towns of course, but some of them came north. The first ones got the best pieces of land, although that wasn't planned. The government didn't even know where the best land was.

"Well, word got back that there was good land to be had, and they came swarming in. No way could the government control them. You should have seen it! They came by the thousands. Some of them spent days in the bus station at Cuiabá, just waiting for a seat.

"Of course the road was terrible then, not tarmacked like it is now. In those days it used to take two weeks or more to get here from Cuiabá. That was in the wet season. The trucks and buses were always getting stuck. I remember we used to have to carry all our food when we traveled, and of course you never knew how long it was going to take you to get anywhere. They say that people used to die on the bus sometimes!

"We had to carry cooking pots and everything. The bus would stop by the side of the road, and we'd all just get out and make ourselves a meal. Often the bus didn't have to stop at all, because it already *was* stopped—behind a long line of vehicles trying to get through the holes. When it got stuck, we'd get out and push, all of us out there in the rain and the mud. Miserable. You can imagine.

"The government did its best to encourage the settlers to grow cash crops. You must have seen the notice at the bus station when you arrived: 'Cacoal: Center of Coffee Production.' Well, people planted coffee and cocoa and sometimes rubber. Some of them did all right, up in Ouro Preto do Oeste, for instance. The soils are excellent there. But in Rondônia only about seventeen percent of the soils are any good, so of course most people ended up on bad land.

"Another thing was that no one had any experience with agriculture in the forestlands—except the *ribeirinhos*. They had a good eye for choosing the best lands. And the settlers came in so fast that we couldn't cope. We had the settlement schemes laid out, but there just wasn't enough land for all those people, and some of them headed off into the forest and carved out a piece of land for themselves. Sometimes they ended up on Indian lands, and then there was trouble. Down toward Costa Marques—there wasn't a road then—there was a settler family who had their place raided by the Indians. Two of their children were killed. Another was kidnapped, and they spent years looking for him. They thought he was in the forest somewhere with the Indians. It wasn't until much later that they found out he'd been dead all along. It turned out to be a tribe that had never been contacted before—the Uru Eu Wau Wau.

"I don't suppose that more than ten percent of the original settlers are still there today. The problem was the soils, you see. Most of them just aren't suitable for agriculture. But it took us a few years to find that out. When you first clear the land, there's still a bit of fertility in it, and the first year's crops do fine. The next year isn't so good, and the third year is often a dead loss. The problem was that nobody realized that, not even the government people—not at the beginning. And there wasn't any support for the settlers, not even seeds or fertilizers.

"One of the toughest things was the transport. They'd put in all those dirt roads, but in the rainy season they turned into seas of mud. It's the same today, although, heaven knows, it's a lot better than it used to be. In the wet season the roads would get so bad that the settlers couldn't begin to get their stuff out to market. And they had trouble with money. A lot of them weren't used to dealing with money, so they'd go and take out big loans from the bank without realizing what they were doing. And of course they couldn't pay. A lot of them lost their land that way. Some of the others would be offered amounts that seemed like a lot to them—but weren't really—and just couldn't resist selling out. Plenty of land grabbers pulled that trick. But some of *them* lost out too. The price of land has dropped a lot around here.

"The tragedy is that so many of the settlers failed. They started out with such high hopes, with great courage, and work! If work alone could have done it, there'd be plenty of rich people around these parts. You see, they thought they could work the same up here as they could in the south. But you can't, not in this climate. They came up here because they had nothing back home, and they were determined to make something for themselves. So sometimes they would clear far more land than they could possibly manage with only their families to work. Most of them had young families, so the children couldn't do much.

"Then there was the malaria. Nobody had thought about that. They got it all the time—still do. Do you know that in Ariquemes, that's just 190 miles north of here, almost half the population has malaria every year? They call it the malaria capital of the world.

"Another disappointment was that even the pastures didn't hold up. Everybody likes to have cattle. It's money in the bank. You can look at your cow and know that if there's any problem you can always sell her. You can turn her into money when you need it. Cows don't require a lot of looking after either—just the thing for a small family. Well, they cleared the land and made pasture, and the grass got invaded by *capoeira* scrub. It's very hard to clear out, and the cattle won't eat it. You'll see a lot of it about—a sure sign of degraded land.

"These days they're abandoning cocoa and coffee. The prices are down, and they're simply too much work. The inputs are expensive too. They're growing subsistence crops instead: rice, beans, and manioc.

"You can't say that Polonoroeste was a success, but it wasn't for lack of trying. Now they're trying to set up another scheme. It's called Planafloro, and they're going to make a real effort to preserve areas that aren't suitable for agriculture and encourage agroforestry instead. They're setting up extractive reserves, trying to manage the forests better, and doing something for the river people. They're concentrating the agriculture on the good lands. They're also going to try to regenerate the degraded areas. Well, I just hope it does better than the last plan. A lot of messed-up land and a lot of disappointed settlers, that's what we got last time around."

I talked to one of the settlers outside the bank in Cacoal. He was in town to collect some cattle food for his dairy herd of thirty-four cows. He told me that his name was Cesar Abrantes de Araujo, he was sixty-four years old, and he had been in Rondônia since 1974. Today he has almost 500 acres near Espigão do Oeste. Besides his cows, he grows corn and beans and has recently started a small plantation of *guaraná*—a popular health drink. He is doing all right.

"You want to know about these settlement schemes? Well, we had to get the land from somewhere, didn't we? There isn't any left down in the south; it's all been bought up by the big companies. It's not as if we're not good farmers. After all, we're the ones who grow all the food that people actually eat. What are the big farmers growing? Soy, for animal feed, and citrus, and beef and broiler chickens. Most of that goes for export.

"All we wanted was a place to be able to plant our crops and bring up our families decently. You would have thought that the government would see that it makes sense to give us good pieces of land. But then, I suppose it did try with the settlement schemes. The idea was all right, but it didn't work for most of us. The soils weren't any good and we didn't get any help with things we needed, like seeds and fertilizers and credit and marketing. And of course it wasn't easy for us to clear the land. We had to cut it and burn it. Waste of good wood, if you ask me, but we didn't have time to wait. We had to get those seeds into the ground. We need the land just as much as the Indians do. After all, we're the ones that are actually growing things. They don't do much, do they? Neither do the rubber tappers, for that matter. If you want food, you'd better get a settler to grow it for you. We know what we're doing."

Some days later we had an opportunity to talk with another settler family. This one was in the neighboring state of Acre.

"I'll take you out to Quinari to meet Lara and Mauro," said my friend Ricardo, as we set off briskly in the stifling midday heat. "There's two buses, one leaves five minutes after the other. We'll try for the first; it's better than the other." He led the way down the hill in Rio Branco, the capital city. The street was jammed with street vendors selling cheap jewelry, garish neon-colored hair ribbons, frilly underwear, single cigarettes, little piles of tired-looking vegetables, gummy chunks of fly-covered coconut candy, and watches smuggled from Bolivia. Everyone was moving slowly in the sticky heat, and it was hard to get through. At the bottom of the hill an iron bridge led over the River Acre. It looked Victorian, but it dated from the 1970s. Beneath it, a large pile of malodorous garbage lay on the riverbank, and further down there was a line of small riverboats. A canoe drifted listlessly downstream, its paddler half asleep. Meanwhile a procession of elderly trucks and buses staggered past, spewing black exhaust.

There was no sign of a bus at the bus stop. "Must have gone already," said Ricardo, philosophically. "Never mind, the other one will be along any minute."

The bus careered up. It certainly wasn't the better bus. The upholstery was torn, the windows were grimy, and the driver clearly thought he was another Ayrton Senna (the world champion Formula One race car driver). He shot around corners, narrowly missed unseeing pedestrians, wove around large holes in the street, screamed to a halt at a police checkpoint, and finally headed off on the road to Xapuri.

"This is a typical settler family. You'll enjoy meeting them," began Ricardo. "They came from Paraná, and got a plot on the Pedro Peixoto scheme. They did well out of it, too. Of course the husband wasn't just a settler; he was a tractor driver, and now he's got his own truck. They'll have plenty of stories to tell."

Ricardo was going to Quinari for the monthly service of the Reformed Lutheran Church, of which he was the pastor. "There aren't too many Lutherans up here," he said, "but they're a good bunch, and hard workers. They're doing fine."

Fifty minutes later the bus pulled into a small town marked "Senador Guiomard." I looked at the signboard in surprise, expecting to be in Quinari.

"Oh, the sign doesn't mean anything," laughed Ricardo, blue eyes squinting from behind his thick glasses. "That's just some politician's idea. The people here call it Quinari. It's the old name, and they're not about to change it just to suit the senator."

We picked our way down a rutted street and past a row of wooden houses with hard-baked earth around them.

"They keep it like that on purpose," said Ricardo, "because of the snakes."

About 500 yards down on the left was a small bar with a large speaker system all set up. Nobody was there. "That belongs to Dona Lara," said Ricardo. "They call it a 'Party Room' so they won't shock their pastor, I suppose. Once I was staying with them after the service, and I asked what time everyone went to bed, just so I could know. Well, they said they'd be up late because it was Saturday night, and then I discovered they had this bar. They were a bit defensive about it and said that I could stay in the house if I'd rather. But I told them I wasn't going to miss out, and we sat up drinking beer until two in the morning. Here we are. Come and meet the family."

The wooden house was spotless. Everything shone from constant sweeping and scrubbing. Dona Lara emerged from the kitchen all smiles. Small and dark, she had neat brown hair and bright blue eyes. Her husband, in his Sunday best, was scrubbed and silent. Rows of identical children, blond and blue-eyed, sat on stools inside the house, swinging their legs. Dona Lara produced a bottle of ice water from the refrigerator, and handed around glass after glass.

"So you want to know about the early days on the settlement scheme?" she began, without preamble. "Well, I reckon you could write a whole book just about us—so many adventures. But everything has worked out for the best. Thank God." She cast a sideways look at the pastor, who returned a wide smile.

"We used to live in Paraná, you see. My husband worked as a tractor driver for one of the big farmers. But he always wanted to have his own place. We used to talk about it sometimes, but of course there wasn't any land to be had in Paraná, not by that time. Lots of small farmers had already moved out. I remember the day he came and said to me, 'Lara, we're off to the Amazon. The boss has bought a place up there, and he wants us to go too. He says there's six months' work for us there, and then we can settle there if we want, or else we can come back down with him. What about it, Lara?'

"I said, 'When do we leave?'

"And he said, 'Monday.' This was Saturday, you understand. I packed up the house all day Sunday; we didn't have much, and only one baby then. On Monday we were ready to go. I didn't even know exactly where we were going or anything, but we climbed into the truck, put our mattresses on the top, took our cooking pots and some food, and off we went to Acre. It was the dry season, so the road wasn't too bad, but even so it took us nine days—nine days bouncing about on top of that truck. I will never forget it, never! But it was fun, because we were off to a new life. We never had any intention of coming back, you see. We were sure it was the big chance for us. And so it was.

"The boss had gone on ahead by plane, so he was there when we arrived in Rio Branco, and he told Mauro that he could get right to work, and that the baby and I could go out to the camp where the workers were living. So we hardly had time to get off one truck, and there we were on another, heading for his farm. Well, it wasn't exactly what you'd call a farm. Not at all what we were used to. It was just a piece of dense jungle at the end of a long muddy road. The truck driver stopped in the middle of nowhere and pointed off to the left. 'It's down there,' he said.

"I couldn't see anything at all, but he showed me a sort of a path, and so I picked up the baby and off I went. I left the mattress and our things right there by the side of the road. I mean, I couldn't carry them, and I didn't think there'd be anyone else around those parts to make off with them. I did put them all out of sight though, just in case, and then I set off down this little muddy trail. My heart was in my mouth, I can tell you. It was so dark inside that forest, and I kept wondering if there were any jaguars in there. 'It's along there,' the truck driver had said. 'You can't miss it.' Well, I was hoping he was right, because if I got myself lost in there, I would have been in quite a state. After a while I found a clear place to sit down. The baby was getting heavy, and I needed a little rest.

"Then, as I was sitting there, I heard something coming through the forest. I thought it was a jaguar, so I jumped up. I wasn't going to let it come up on me like that. And I shouted as loud as I could. I said, 'You're not going to get me, you old cat,' or something like that. Imagine my surprise when along comes this old man on a mule. Well, I felt like a fool then, but I don't think he heard what I said. Or maybe he couldn't understand it. They speak very funny around here, as you've probably noticed. Well, this old man said that I could take a ride on the mule, and he told me that the camp wasn't far ahead at all. So up I climbed, feeling just like Mary and the baby Jesus, and that's how we arrived at the camp.

"Well, it didn't look much, I can tell you. Just a shelter made out of plastic. And there wasn't a soul about. But it was obvious that someone lived there, because there was a lot of stuff around the place. So I went in and settled down in a corner, and took out the bit of food I'd brought. I found a pot and made a fire, and soon I had something hot for us to eat. That made me feel better.

"Later on the men came back. They looked like a rough lot, and I was a bit scared at first, being the only woman and all, but they were kind to me, and one of them volunteered to go back and get our things, and soon we were all drinking coffee together as if we'd known each other all our lives. After a while I heard the sound of a tractor. That was a surprise, since there weren't any roads. And then along comes my man, sitting right up there on the tractor, making a track as he goes along. Well, I was glad to see him, I can tell you!

"We stayed there a bit, and then we got our own piece of land on one of the settlement schemes. My husband was thrilled to have his own place at last, although it wasn't easy.

"They called it Pedro Peixoto. It had been an old rubber place, and the owner had gone bust and sold out. Some of the rubber tappers were trying to settle there, but it was awfully hard for them. The plots of land were so small—125 to 250 acres—not what they'd been used to. And they didn't have any idea about growing things. You couldn't expect them to, not after all those years doing nothing but tapping the rubber and collecting nuts.

"Well, the first thing we had to do was to clear the place. We had a nice little patch of land, and there was plenty of water, at least in the wet season. So we put up a sort of a shack to start with, just palm thatch and black plastic. We thought it was more important to get the place cleared and the crops planted, and then we'd build our house in peace. Some of the other settlers did it the other way around, but they missed the planting season.

"Most of them had bigger families than we did. I think we were among the youngest. We didn't clear much that first year. I remember that Mauro went in with an ax, cutting and clearing a bit, and then we burned it. *That* was exciting, seeing all that forest going up in flames, although I did hope that the fire wasn't going to get our house! Not that it looked much better after the fire—lots of ash everywhere, and these big tree trunks standing there half burned. It gave me the creeps, sometimes. Not like the land in Paraná at all.

"After that, we cleared a bit more, we made holes there among the burned tree trunks—they were too big to move—and then we planted. We started by putting in corn and a bit of rice. And I planted my garden. People here, they don't do that, I don't know whether you've noticed. They're very lazy in these parts. All they plant is a few onions and some coriander. They put it in old wash pans or wooden boxes raised off the ground. They say you have to do that to keep the wild animals and the bugs and pests out. Well, I was determined to grow my garden the way I used to do it in Paraná, but it didn't really do. I planted on the right moon, and everything looked good to start with. But then it all seemed to get the wilt, or something, and hardly anything came out right. After all that work it was heartbreaking.

"Oh, excuse me a minute. I think it's time to go to the service now. I can tell you a lot more later, if you're interested. More water, pastor?"

She graciously disengaged herself, polished up the children, and ushered everyone out to the back. In the yard was an ancient truck, immaculately clean and obviously much loved. Dona Lara handed up all the stools from the house, the children scrambled aboard, and the truck lurched off. The road was narrow and viciously rutted, but the big truck sailed easily over the bumps.

There was time to examine the surroundings. Small wooden houses crouched on their patches of bare earth. Sometimes we could see a family cow tethered to a stake by the roadside. Dogs ran out at the truck, snarling. Children stared from the porches of their houses.

The church was a small wooden building surrounded by neatly cleared land. Eight or nine people were already there. They shook my hand politely and introduced themselves: Anton, Ira, Karl, Maria, Johann. The German names mingled oddly with their softer Latin counterparts. Thirteen children bowed gravely, as blond and well turned-out as those in any classroom in northern Europe. The church was bare inside except for a row of wooden benches. Ricardo stood up, smiled broadly, and began.

After the service, a meeting of the church was called. Each man gave his opinion quietly and in turn. The women also spoke, although deferentially, and only after all the men had expressed their opinions.

By the end of the meeting, Dona Lara's husband, Mauro, had got over his initial reserve and was eager to tell us what he thought of Acre. "Do I miss Paraná? Oh yes, sometimes. See that orange tree over there? Hardly any fruit on it at all. Well, in Paraná you can grow anything. Here things don't do as well, and I don't know why. You'd think anything would grow up here in this jungle. But then sometimes I hear there's a drought back in Paraná, and I'm glad I'm up here. We've always got enough water in Acre. At least, *we* have. Some of our neighbors in Pedro Peixoto cut all the trees around the water holes, and now the water's dried up. I would never cut any trees that I didn't have to. My father taught me that. And we never ran out of water. Not on our place."

Later on, over the *chimarrão*, the communal gourd of bitter *mate* (a kind of tea) so beloved by people from the south, Dona Lara continued her story.

"We're not living out at the colony now, as you can see. One of our neighbors looks after the place for us, but we'll be going out there on Tuesday for a few days, and you'd be most welcome to come if you like. We were luckier than most, because Mauro had a bit of money put away from his job when we started. So after a while he was able to lay hands on this truck, and then he started hauling things for people. There's a great shortage of transport in these parts, so we're doing all right now.

"What gave him the idea was the *marreteiros.* That's the name they give to the traders. Those first few years, we used to grow our crops all right—rice, corn, beans, manioc, and coffee—but when the time came to sell, we used to have terrible problems because the roads were so dreadful. The government was supposed to look after them, but it never did anything—still doesn't. They're a scandal, the roads in this place. I mean, fancy having a state that isn't even connected to the rest of the country by a tarmac road!

"So we had to sell to the traders. And they'd pay us whatever price they fancied. They used to bring us supplies too. They charged two or three times what you would pay in the town, but we didn't have any option, did we? The rubber tappers told us that they'd always done that, but what could they do? Nothing, they said. 'Nothing? We're not going to do nothing,' I said. 'We'll have it out with them.' So we did. We told them straight out: 'We know you're overcharging us, and we're not standing for it.' Well, that gave them a bit of a surprise, and they started making all sorts of excuses, saying that their costs were high, and that the trucks were expensive to maintain, and all that. But it didn't cut any ice with us.

"We thought we'd ask the government people to lend us a truck so that we could do our own trading, but the problem was the road. It was in such bad shape that they couldn't get anything in to us. That was the fault of the *marreteiros* too. They would come through in the rainy season and leave the road a terrible mess. Nothing could get through after they'd got themselves stuck in the mud and winched themselves out.

"But we didn't give up. We formed a settlers' association. Not all the settlers joined it, but most did, especially the ones from the south. Southerners are always more advanced than these people up here, you see. I can't help it; it's true. And I suppose it isn't entirely their fault, stuck up here at the back of beyond. Anyway, we decided that we wouldn't let the *marreteiros* keep on messing up our road like that. But they said that it wasn't their fault, and they had to get through, and what did we expect them to do about it? They said that the rubber tappers would starve if they didn't get their supplies.

"Well, of course we didn't want that, but we couldn't let the road get in that sort of state either. We kept having to work on it ourselves, and we just didn't have the time to do that. So we put a barrier across the road, just outside our house. And when a *marreteiro* came along, I went out and talked to him. 'I'm afraid you can't go through today,' I said, all nice and polite. 'The road will get into a mess if you do, and then we won't be able to use it. But you can stay here with us until it gets a bit drier, and we'll give you something to eat. If it's dry tomorrow, you can go in there, and it'll be better for all of us. Our road won't get damaged, and you won't have to waste time getting stuck in the mud.'

"They didn't like *that* very much, but in the end they came around to it, and they stayed with us. Good friends we made with some of them. And when the road was a bit better, we went to the town and borrowed a truck from the government. That way we could take our own stuff out and sell it for a better price.

"Things got much easier after that. And later on Mauro and I managed to buy our own truck, and we leased it to the settlers' association. And then we decided to leave the colony and move somewhere a bit more central.

"But those were good days out on the colony, and we made friends with all the neighbors. The ones right next to us had been rubber tappers before. We had our ups and downs with them, as you can imagine. But it worked out all right. We helped them a bit with the farming, which they didn't know much about, except for manioc. They were very good with manioc and that was a help to us, because we hadn't any experience in growing the stuff. And then we built our house—a nice wooden house, you'll see it for yourself—almost like the house we used to have back home. Oh, dear! Mustn't call it home must I? This is home now.

"At first there wasn't a school out there, but when our eldest got to be seven or eight, we thought he must have somewhere to learn to read and write, otherwise he'd end up no better than those rubber tappers, if you know what I mean. And the government did put in a school. It wasn't a very good one, but it was a start. They had trouble getting teachers who wanted to live out there—it's a long way out—but in the end we got a really good one. Maria Teresa, her name is. She's still there, and everyone loves her.

"Of course I had my hens, and I used to give her a nice chicken whenever I could, or a few eggs. And we'd fatten a pig and sell off half to our neighbors. Well, not exactly sell. We used to trade it for something else: a bag of beans, some vegetables, a bottle of honey, sometimes a few days' help in the fields. After a while we made a little patch of pasture and then we had an argument about it. I wanted a cow. We could use the milk, I remember I said to Mauro, and we could raise a calf for meat. Well, he wanted to have a horse. He was fed up with not having any transport. So we got a horse, and then we got a cow too, and everybody was happy.

"One year a little beetle came into the pasture and ate it all up, just like the locusts in the Bible. Well, that was a bad moment, I can tell you. All the neighbors had the same trouble. We had to sell off the cow. We held onto the horse though, and just grubbed around for forage for her. Mauro wasn't going to give *her* up, not after we'd got a cart and all. After that we planted a different type of grass, and we never had that problem again.

"They were tough, those early years, but they were fun. And you don't get something for nothing, do you?"

Back in Porto Velho, we went to the governor's office to find out what state policy was regarding the settlement schemes. The governor's chief private secretary met us and conducted us to his comfortable air-conditioned office.

"We've had a lot of grief about this Polonoroeste project," he laughed disarmingly. "But you have to try to remember the background. Those were heady days, back in the early 1970s. Brazil was experiencing a big boom, the generals were in charge, and everything seemed possible. There'd already been several private colonization schemes in this area, you know. They were started up in the 1960s, when the road first went in. Pretty dismal they were too. So the government felt that it could do a better job.

"What went wrong was that nobody had any idea what the soils were like. Back then people still imagined that soils that support such a lush stand of forest must be fertile. It wasn't until later that we learned differently.

"The settlement schemes were laid out by bureaucrats who didn't pay any attention to the topography of the place. The plots were arranged in identical rectangles, and of course some of them were completely flooded; others didn't have a drop of water!

"We totally underestimated the number of people willing to come up here and make a new life for themselves. We were caught completely unprepared, and of course we didn't have enough people or the resources to cope. And we didn't have the experience in agricultural practices on these sorts of soils. We were working in the dark.

"They were wildly exciting days. All those people coming to the promised land! It was only later that we began to run into problems. Then the whole ecology business started up, and suddenly people on the other side of the world were making a fuss about burning the forest, as though it belonged to them!

"But we did achieve a lot. I'd say that in the early part of the 1980s we did wonders. We improved the roads and set up local communities, schools, and health posts. We did all those good things, but we didn't really get to the root of the problem.

"I don't know if you're familiar with the work of Professor Samuel Benchimol? His theory is that sustainable development has to be based on three things: it has to be economically sound, ecologically balanced, and socially just. Well, in order to fulfill these criteria, we realized that we needed much more information about the different types of ecosystems. We needed to get some zoning done so that we could see how to make the best possible use of the land.

"We're in a better position now to analyze just what went wrong—and right too. It wasn't all disaster! But we need to take steps to make sure that the next twenty years are better planned.

There's a real danger in Rondônia that the settlers will sell out to the big ranchers and either go off to the *garimpo* or leave the state altogether. We don't have any figures, but we do know that people are starting to pack up and leave. Sixty-three percent of the original settlement lands have already been abandoned. If we don't do something, the ranchers will come in and gobble them all up.

"We need to put our farming on a sound economic footing. And we need to increase production. It's absurd that we should be importing so much food from the south. Have you any idea what it costs to ship everything nearly 2,500 miles up here?

"Let me tell you a bit about our development plan. It's called Planafloro, and we're very excited about it. It's not often that you get the chance to set up a new state, just like that. And even less often do you have a second chance! Our number one priority is to come up with a model of sustainable development. We want to improve our production, protect our environment, and provide better living conditions for our people.

"We've divided the state up into six zones. The first is based along the BR-364. It's where the settlement schemes are, and it serves a population of 930,000—most of the inhabitants of the state, in fact. Over half the population lives in the rural areas. It covers an area of almost fifteen million acres.

"The emphasis in Zone 1 is on improved agricultural production. We want our farmers to make a better living. We'll do this by introducing more lucrative crops—perennial crops rather than subsistence ones—and recuperating degraded lands so they can be put to productive use. It'll come with a package of agricultural extension and research, rural credit, electrification, sanitation, health, and education.

"Zone 2 is half the size—7.5 million acres. The population is 449,000, and most of them live in the towns. The soils aren't so good in this area. At present they're growing subsistence crops along with a little coffee. Here's where we'd like to concentrate on agroforestry—planting rubber and coffee together, for example. We also plan to upgrade the *capoeiras,* make better use of the forest, install better extension and cooperative services, and see if we can't introduce the use of animals for traction.

"The next zone is the riverine zone—1.2 million acres and about 14,000 people. At present they live from fishing, extraction, gold mining, and a little primitive agriculture on the riverbanks. Here we'll concentrate on technical assistance with agriculture and fishing and help with credits and cooperatives. It's essential to improve the river transport system, since that's all they've got. Health and education come in there too, of course.

"Zone 4 is the extractive zone. It covers 8.6 million acres and serves 2,500 people. They live by rubber tapping and collecting nuts. We plan to set up five extractive reserves, and settle another 500 rubber tappers and their families. In order to make a go of it, we'll have to step up the production of rubber and other forest products and place more emphasis on things like gums, oils, essences, roots, and fruits. We have to look after both the forests and the fauna and help out with community organization, extension, health, and education.

"Zone 5 is managed forest—8.6 million acres. We'll be trying to figure out the best development model for sustainable forestry. We'll start by making an inventory; then we'll work on better ways of protecting the forest, managing it, and marketing the lumber.

"Zone 6 is the area of permanent preservation. It covers 16 million acres and serves 5,000 people, mostly indigenous. The idea is to set up biological reserves, protect Indian lands, and set aside areas for two hydroelectric plants. We plan to leave the place untouched, as far as possible, but it'll be working for its living. We'll be producing seedlings, researching sustainable forestry, monitoring environmental pollution, protecting the watersheds, and setting up ecotourism.

"That's the shape of things to come. It's our big chance to make something out of these forestlands and use them in the best way possible for the benefit of the people who live there. Quite a challenge, isn't it?"

8

RANCHERS

Nothing shall stop me in this movement which is in the highest task of civilizing man; to conquer and dominate the valleys of the great equatorial torrents, transforming their blind force and their extraordinary energy into disciplined fertility. The Amazon . . . shall become a chapter in the history of civilization.
—President Getulio Vargas, 1940

I had expected Fazenda Vista Alegre to be something grander. The ranch house in Xapuri, Acre, is small and shabby. The rooms are a clutter of hammocks and hats, rifles and saddles, empty liquor bottles and cigarette butts. The toilet doesn't flush, there's no water in the taps, and the kitchen—really just an enclosed space at the back—is decorated with blackened pots of rice and beans, sacks of weevily manioc flour, salt, onions, coffee, dried meat, and curing hides. The generator has broken down, and our supper of fish and rice is served by candlelight.

"Well," says the rancher, "You wanted to see the *fazenda*. I don't live here, of course, and the peons don't look after anything properly. I suppose you're wondering what in the world made me leave my home state and come up to this corner of the Wild West? The challenge, I think. I figured that I could make something out of all this space. My dad's place in Minas is just too small.

"I came to Acre fifteen years ago. They were desperate to get people up here in those days. It was pretty rough, I can tell you. But a few of us thought like I did, and we came in here to make a go of it.

"We got a lot of help. The state couldn't do too much for us: interest-free start-up loans, tax exemptions, you name it, we had it. All we had to do was start knocking that forest down. The governor talked of cutting a road through to the Pacific, and we had visions of selling our beef to the Far East. Acre wasn't going to be dependent on the south of Brazil; we were going to be spearheading Amazon development. Pretty heady stuff! And it's going to happen. Once that road goes in, there won't be anything to stop us.

"It was easy to get started. The land cost practically nothing, and there was all that cheap money. I was lucky with this place, because I was able to harvest a lot of good wood, and that saved me a bundle. After selling the wood, I had to clear the land. No bulldozers were available, so we used chain-saw gangs. It wasn't easy to get the labor, though. The *caboclos* in Acre are pretty independent, and they're not about to work any harder than they have to. I found it best to recruit my workers from down south, although you have to pay them more, of course.

"Then you set the fire. That's the skilled part. There's been a lot of fuss lately about burning the forest, but everyone knows that it's the First World, not us, that's responsible for the greenhouse effect. It's the carbon emissions from all their cars. The amount generated by burning the forest is minuscule by comparison.

"There's something elemental about firing the forest. I suppose it has to do with making a home for your family and taming the wilderness. But you have to know what you're doing. You don't want to make a fire storm. You clear what you can first. Then you burn it, but it's got to be carefully controlled. After that you can go ahead and plant the grass. Manual planting is probably the most effective method under these conditions. Then it's time for a second burn—to keep the weeds under control. This one doesn't affect the grass seed, if you do it right. You have to keep on top of those weeds. They're the devil. Turn your back and they're over your head.

"After the pasture is formed, all you have to do is keep it clean. We send in teams to clear it out. I tried aerial spraying, but it doesn't pay. You can use herbicides too. You do whatever it takes to stay ahead. The pastures look wonderful to start with, but that's because of the residual fertility in the soil. It's deceptive. After five or six years the pastures are pretty well shot, and even if you throw fertilizer at them, they don't respond. It's probably cheaper to clear new pasture at that stage, especially if you can get interest-free loans.

"Most of us around here bought in on the hope that the Pacific Road would go through this way. Of course people who bought land on the Cruzeiro road were hoping the same thing! But this is still a better location, because at least our road is passable, whereas theirs isn't.

"We did run into a bunch of troublemakers, though, particularly in the Xapuri area. We hadn't expected the rubber tappers to give us so much grief. To tell you the truth, when I came up here, I didn't even know there *were* any rubber tappers living in here. I mean, I'd read about them in history books, but I couldn't imagine anyone would still want to live that way in this day and age. And there was a lot of confusion over land titles. I paid good money for this place, and I wouldn't want to do anyone out of their land. I'm as honest as the next man. But the land titling in Acre is absolutely chaotic. There's hardly a clean title in the entire state. Half the problem is that the place has been under so many different jurisdictions. To start with, of course, Acre was Bolivian, and there are still some titles dating from those days. Then it became independent, and so they issued a whole lot more titles. There are titles dating from the days when Acre was a territory, and a whole lot more were issued when it became a state. Nobody knows where the hell they are. Not that the rubber tappers ever had title anyway. They had land-use rights, that's all. Usufruct, they call it.

"Well, after I'd bought this place, I suddenly discovered a whole lot of rubber tappers were trying to stop me taking possession of it, saying that it was theirs and that I had no right to cut down the trees. No right to do what I wanted with my own land? Well, that was a bit of a surprise, as you can imagine!

"Now I'm not one to come in with the strong-arm boys. I believe in settling things in a peaceful manner. Those who live by the sword will die by the sword, that's what it says somewhere, doesn't it? At the same time, I can't have this bunch of peasants interfering with my development plans, can I? So I got together with their leaders. I offered them plots of land elsewhere. It wasn't as though there wasn't plenty of land for all of us. It's just a question of being rational, that's all. But they didn't want *those* plots; said that there wasn't enough rubber, and that each family needed 450 to 750 acres. Where the hell was I going to put my cattle?

"And then they started on this business of 'peaceful protests.' They're a bunch of communists, if you ask me. They'd get a whole gang of people together, including women and children, and they'd walk in and frighten off my workers. Not forcibly. They were much too clever for that. They'd just go in and persuade them not to cut the trees. So of course my boys would stop. They weren't about to get themselves involved in any trouble.

"You must have heard about those little standoffs. But I'll bet you've never heard it from the landowners' point of view! There's people trying to make out that Chico Mendes was some sort of saint. He was nothing more than a nuisance, a communist agitator. I had to go to court to get the police to throw him and his men off my land. It was all a great waste of time, particularly as I nearly always ended up clearing the forest anyway."

Next morning everyone was stirring well before dawn. "Got to slaughter a couple of steers and take them back with us," our host cheerfully informed us. Beneath our hammocks a pair of large dogs had started their morning playtime, chasing each other around and around playing tug-of-war with one of my socks. As if on cue from some invisible conductor, the birds began a lusty morning chorus. A couple of peons shouldered their rifles and stumbled sleepily into the morning chill. Somebody had made a lethally strong brew of coffee, and we gulped it down.

As the mist rose, we could see blackened tree stumps rising out of lush green pastures. "See those fields?" said the rancher. "Lovely, aren't they? We made them just last year." Great herds of white cattle were scattered over the fields as far as the eye could see. It was a picture of rural innocence, yet indelibly associated in our minds with ruin and destruction.

A gang of peons rode up, spurs jingling, harnesses heavy with silver rings. On the horizon the jungle appeared sparse and defeated. Later we would see great areas of impenetrable *capoeira*, a sort of revenge. We collected the two bloody steer carcasses and drove back to town in silence.

We weren't at all sure what to make of our visit to the ranch. Had it been situated in Wyoming, for example, would we have felt so uneasy about it? If not, why not? The Wyoming ranch would have displaced prairie land and prairie dwellers, just as the Amazon ranch had displaced forestland and forest people. After all, the government of Brazil had attempted to develop its frontier in exactly the same way as the government of the United States had done 150 years earlier. In a world reared on Western movies where the Marlboro-smoking cowboy tames the frontier, it was an attractive model.

The United States became the richest and most powerful nation in the world by exploiting its natural resources and riding roughshod over its native population. Why should Brazil not follow suit? And what can the Europeans reasonably say to Brazil about cutting the Amazon jungle, when they have not only destroyed much of their own forest but have also become rich and influential in the bargain? England, one of Brazil's most vociferous critics, has lost forty-nine percent of its own forest cover, yet has a gross domestic product (GDP) of $11,770 per capita. Switzerland, with the same forest loss, has a GDP of more than twice that. Whereas Brazil, the country with the richest resource base in the world and the largest area of forest, has a GDP of only $2,250.

The way in which the Brazilian government opened up the Amazon for development was also, on the face of it, perfectly rational. At the time, the forest was not seen as a rich resource but as an underutilized space that should be occupied. Here's how the strategy went: the government had a large area to develop. If it provided the right incentives, the multinationals and the big businesspeople from the south would do the job for it. The government's first priority was the cattle ranchers, followed by agriculture and then industry. If it provided generous tax rebates and financial incentives, the ranchers would underwrite the cost of frontier development, create employment, and supply products for export. It was a developer's dream.

From the point of view of the businesspeople, this deal was too good to pass up. The land was dirt cheap, and development costs were largely borne by the state. But, as everyone discovered, it's extremely difficult to set up a ranch in the Amazon. There's a constant battle against the jungle. Pastures deteriorate quickly, and stocking rates are low. Realistically, ranchers can expect to produce about 270 pounds of beef per acre of pasture per year, so nobody is going to make a fortune out of beef. Those who made fortunes did so from tax breaks and other financial perks, finding their land appreciating by as much as 1,000 percent.

Thirty years after the first ranches opening up, what are the results? Not fields full of fat cattle, not rich revenues from the export of Brazilian beef. The government has now withdrawn from the subsidy program and provides only minimal support for existing ranches, which cover almost 30 million acres throughout Amazônia. But the place *has* developed. Where there was once an impenetrable jungle inhabited by a few Indians and *caboclos*, there's now a whole new frontier waiting to take off.

Ecologists argue that ranching is an inefficient way of using the forest. They tell us that in order to make $1 million a year from cattle in Amazônia, you need to cut about thirty-eight square miles of forest; to make the equivalent money out of a good stand of timber, you need to cut less than one square mile; and out of mining a mere 0.006 square miles. They also point out that almost two million acres of forest have been knocked down in order to create great stretches of largely unproductive pasture, and the expected international market for Brazilian beef never materialized. Nor did the beef. The ranches still don't produce enough to satisfy local demand; in fact, Amazônia is a net importer of beef. To be fair, however, all these arguments have the benefit of hindsight. When the ranching program began, most experts believed that the area could and should become the breadbasket of South America.

Sociologists point out that massive land consolidation in the hands of a few rich businesspeople will do nothing to solve Brazil's social problems. Land in the Amazon should have been distributed to the landless, they say. That is another story, one that the government has also tried, as we saw in the last chapter.

To all this the ranchers counter that they are the true pioneers, the founding fathers of the New West. They point out that when they set up their ranches, nobody knew how the pastures would fare. They say that it was altogether reasonable to expect the Amazon to support a good population of cattle, thereby providing a large source of beef for both internal and export markets. They mention that even such an experienced and canny businessman as Daniel K. Ludwig believed that the region could feed the world. They suggest that a conspiracy exists among the ecologists, the church, and the unions to portray the ranchers as the villains of Amazônia. They add that all these factions are, in fact, being manipulated by international interests. They conclude that the ranchers are being unfairly cast as the chief offenders, when they are really the heroes of the frontier.

We decided to talk to some other cattlemen. "Go and have a chat with Sidney," said our friends in Rio Branco, exchanging glances. "If you can get him to see you."

Sidney has an office in an air-conditioned block just opposite one of Rio Branco's favorite bars. A busy man, he is not enthusiastic about giving interviews. He has strong feelings about outsiders who come up to Acre poking their noses into local affairs, especially in the aftermath of the Chico Mendes affair. But on this occasion his natural good manners prevailed and he agreed, albeit grudgingly, to talk. His set jaw, however, betrayed his determination not to give an inch more than was strictly necessary.

A fleshy forty-year-old, he was prickly and defensive. He sat behind a large desk. In front of him was a map of one section of his property, a trophy or two, and a collection of miniature models of earth-moving equipment. At one stage during our conversation his small son came in, and Sidney softened noticeably. He called for chilled soda, and even consented to demonstrate the large, silver-embellished horn used by cowboys when they are moving big herds of cattle.

"Well, I don't know exactly what you're looking for. The big bad wolf, perhaps? I don't have a lot of time for people who come up here with their minds already made up. You wouldn't believe the stuff people write about us ranchers. You'd think we eat Indian babies or something." He glared at us and then continued, visibly controlling himself.

"I'm a businessman, first and foremost. My business is cattle. I believe that Acre is excellently suited to cattle raising. I have been here eighteen years, and so far as I can see, it is the only thing that does well here. I have [here he paused to make a calculation on his machine] 98,000 acres, of which 12,000 are under pasture. The rest is forest. I run about 6,000 head of Nelore cattle.

"We buy female calves and breed them at two years old. They have their calves at three, and in another three years that steer will be around 600 pounds. We sell them then, right out of the fields.

"I employ somewhere in the neighborhood of a hundred men—more when required. The cattle are divided up into herds of 500. Each herd has three men taking care of it. The other hands are working on the pastures, the fencing, and so on. And then there's maintenance of the roads. That's the major problem: access. That and the expense of making the pastures. But the price of land is low, so it's worth it. And I believe that Acre is going to go places. When they put the road in, we're really going to take off.

"Do you know what I do for fun? I raise quarter horses. I imported the brood mares from the States. Bulldog quarter horses, they are—wonderful with cattle. I have about a hundred. Can't raise them fast enough to sell. Everybody here in Acre wants one.

"So that's how I run my business. If anyone could show me a better way to make money out of this jungle, I'd give it a try. I don't like cutting the forest any more than you do. For one thing, it's hard work. But as far as I can see, the only thing that works here is cattle."

At this point, one of Sidney's colleagues entered the room and Sidney hailed him briskly. "This is Chico. You can interrogate him now," he said with a faint smile. Excusing himself, he hurried out.

Chico was younger, blond, tanned—a good-looking man, and he knew it. He wore boots with just a touch of designer mud on them. "Well, I suppose Sidney has been giving you the party line," he smiled. "If there's one thing Sidney hates worse than a writer, it's a foreigner! I'm surprised he agreed to talk to you. I think he's convinced he's never going to get a fair hearing, and he doesn't see why he should have to defend himself. We don't usually get good press you know.

"Well, never mind Sidney. Let me tell you what *I* think. I came up here five years ago from São Paulo state. I'll tell you something. This place has got huge potential. Really good soils. Best soils in Amazônia, I think. They did some tests the other day, and they figure the soils are ninety percent fertile.

"I've tried planting all sorts of things, all native forest stuff: cocoa, *guaraná*, rubber, coffee. Yet none of them has done as well as I hoped. Take the *guaraná*, for instance: the best-yielding varieties are the most susceptible to pests. The ones that are the most resistant are the low yielders. I haven't come up with the right variety yet. But every year they do well enough to make you think that perhaps next season. . . . You know how it is?

"In the end it may just have to be cows. *Everyone* likes cows. Why, even the smallest settler has one or two, even the rubber tappers. Mind you, those rubber tappers. . . . I don't know what they've told you, but I'd say they are being manipulated by the church to get money out of the Americans. In fact the ecologists are too, although they think they're being so clever. You see, it isn't in the interest of the Americans to let Brazil develop all this area. So they're pretending to be concerned about the environment and about the Indians, when all they really want to do is make the whole place into a reserve so we can't touch what's in there."

While Chico was talking a third rancher appeared, older than the other two, expensively dressed, full of Latin charm. He introduced himself. "I'm Dirceu Zamora, Sidney's brother. I'm in the business too. Like he says, cattle are the only thing that do well here in Acre. When we get the road, you'll see how this place will come on. Already it's God's own country. We've got the climate, we've got the location, we've got people here with the vision to make it work. And it's quiet around here. You don't get people squabbling about the land, like they do over in Pará. You don't get people rushing around and shooting one another. Not in Acre."

We later learned that Dirceu is the head of the UDR, the right-wing union of ranchers and big landowners that is suspected of being involved in the murder of many rural leaders, including Chico Mendes. But he didn't mention that.

Of all the people of the Amazon, the most educated and the most articulate are the ranchers. They do not speak with the hesitant voices of those who live in the forest, but with the confidence of men who are at home in the air-conditioned offices of São Paulo and the country clubs of Rio de Janeiro. They take their families on vacation to places like Disneyland and Aspen, Colorado.

The ranchers come to Amazônia for fun, for adventure, and for money. They regard the area as land that is not being properly used. (We should note here that they see the forest as land, not as trees.) They do not see how Brazil can afford to let this land lie idle for the benefit of a handful of Indians and a few other people who eke out some miserable existence tapping rubber, collecting nuts, and hunting and fishing. Brazil needs to progress, and in order to progress it must develop its greatest asset: Amazônia. And this means developing it in a rational twentieth-century fashion, untrammeled by anachronistic life styles and by sentimental foreigners or left-wing liberals who regard the forest as a zoological garden for their private enjoyment. Amazônia must be developed, they say, and the ranchers alone have the brains, the guts and the cash to do it. They are the heroes of the new frontier.

Although Rondônia has several very large landowners, their holdings cannot compare with those of their neighbors in Acre. In the 1970s, the governor of Acre did everything in his power to make sure that huge chunks of the state were sold off. In some municipalities the government announced—with no trace of irony—that over 100 percent of the land had been sold.

The list of Acre's biggest landowners makes instructive reading: Acre's largest landowner owns 2.4 million acres. He does nothing with the land, partly because he does not hold clear title. Nor is he alone in this. Eighty percent of the lands in Acre are in dispute because of the chaotic titling system. In addition, bribery, corruption, and general confusion abound. The following list gives some indication of the size of the properties (figures are approximate):

- Manuel Meirrelles de Queiroz—2.4 million acres
- Pedro Dotto—1.9 million acres
- Jorge Wolney Atulla—1.0 million acres
- Senator Altevir Leal—655,000 acres
- Joel Tavares de Couto—370,000 acres
- José Tavares de Couto—356,000 acres

Only one subject brings shivers to the spines of people who own land on this scale. That is the subject, rather feebly raised from time to time by a succession of reluctant governments, of land reform. For a moment in 1985 it really looked as though something might be done about land reform. The landowners were quick to respond to the threat to their holdings by forming a union.

Founded by Ronaldo Caiado, a surgeon from Brasília, the ranchers' union started with a membership of 2,000. Among them they owned *a total of ninety-three million cattle*. The UDR, Democratic Rural Union, began ostensibly as a club, emphasizing the homely values of the cowboy and the frontiersman. Its members presented themselves as the vanguard of a mass movement in rural Brazil that sought to promote the trinity of tradition, family, and property. Their meetings were characterized by cattle auctions, barbecues, and country music.

Then they began to move into politics. First, they came out against the proposed land reform, arguing that it would put land into the hands of uneducated farmers who were incapable of using it properly. (This argument conveniently ignores the fact that smallholders produce eighty percent of Brazil's food on twelve percent of the land.) The UDR next started to raise money by auctioning cattle, announcing that the profits would be used for political lobbying. Subsequently, the union admitted to purchasing firearms, for distribution among its members so that they could "defend their property." Salvador Farina, a UDR member from Goiás, is quoted as saying, "Today I think we can say that, yes, we have bought weapons with the money from the cattle auctions. Today we have more than 70,000 guns. One for every man in the UDR, men who decided to stop being left out of our country's history."

Today the UDR has 200,000 members and 359 regional divisions. Its principal achievement has been to water down the government's hesitant attempts at land reform. But there is another, more sinister side to the UDR. It is generally held responsible for the violence taking place in the Amazon land wars. There is a strong likelihood that some of its members were involved in the death of Chico Mendes, among innumerable others. These men are rich and powerful, accustomed to getting their way. Life is cheap in the Amazon. And the stakes are high.

Carlos Terra is a businessman from Rio who ranches in Rondônia. He too is a passionate defender of the rights of the cattlemen to develop the Amazon. Like many of his colleagues, Terra's attitude is a mixture of pride and dismay at the way things have turned out. "It's no business of yours to interfere in our affairs," he says defensively.

"Some people say that Amazônia is an ecological sanctuary and must remain untouched," he continues, "just as if it were a historic house. They talk about those of us who work here as though we are nothing but villains.

"Do you know that I've been in the Amazon for twenty years? And I'll tell you something, I don't regret a single thing that I've done. I'm *proud* of it! I wouldn't undo the cutting of the forest, nor the burnings. There's no other way to beat it. You've got to be tough with it. I must have knocked down 50,000 acres, so I know what I'm talking about.

"It's not as if I'm in favor of destroying the forest. I'm in favor of developing it rationally. After all, Amazônia *has* to be exploited. And there's a lot of misconceptions about the whole thing. Contrary to what people think, if you cut a bit of the forest, it isn't necessarily going to end up as a desert. It's just a question of cutting the right bit. It's no good cutting and planting and then finding out afterwards that the soil is no good. That's why this new zoning in Rondônia is going to be such a good thing. I'm opening up a *fazenda* down in the Guaporé valley. I'm having nothing but success. And there are others following my example—all experienced ranchers, hard workers, and good Brazilians.

"Some people try and make out that we're doing our best to wipe out the forest and kill off all the animals. That's not it at all. We're in here because we feel we can do something useful. God knows, Brazil needs people like us."

9

RUBBER TAPPERS

My life began just like that of all rubber tappers, as a virtual slave bound to do the bidding of his master. I started work at nine years old, and like my father before me, instead of learning my ABC's I learned how to extract latex from the rubber tree.

—Chico Mendes, "O Testamento
do Homem da Floresta," 1989

It was a hot afternoon in Plácido de Castro, Acre, as we trudged into the forest to talk to the rubber tappers. The path was bright with butterflies—neon blue, orange and black, white and yellow. The trees soared so high above us that we could scarcely see their crowns. The forest was cool and pleasant. From time to time we passed a rubber tree, its swollen belly ridged with the scars of old cuts. Our companions were moving along at a fast trot, and we were conscious of the fact that however quickly we walked, we were still holding them up. They had asked us, most courteously, if we would like to lead the way. "Just keep straight," they said, "You can't get lost." But our inexperienced eyes could not differentiate among the maze-like little paths, and we frequently stumbled off in the wrong direction, only to discover that we were on a trail leading nowhere.

We had met Dona Rosane and her son Chico at the trading post, and they had immediately offered to take us home with them. "You can stay with us tonight," said Dona Rosane, kindly, "and tomorrow I'll take you to visit some of the neighbors." She tripped lightly through the forest, seemingly unencumbered by the big shiny washbasin she carried on her back. Chico was carrying a large sack of provisions. My backpack felt heavier than I had remembered, and it was horribly hot.

It was a relief to get to the first clearing and stop for water. In front of us was a comfortable, airy house on stilts. It was entirely constructed of saplings and had a thatched roof. It opened onto a cool veranda, where an inert body was sleeping in a hammock. Repressing a pang of envy, I followed Dona Rosane into the kitchen, which had a gas ring, a wood stove, and shelves neatly stacked with glasses and plates. The tapper's wife served us glass after glass of water from the filter. The men were out, and she complained of being tired. She looked ill.

The afternoon storm was threatening, so we had to speed on. Chico commanded us from the back, indicating a series of short-cuts that became progressively more difficult. Huge fallen trunks had to be scrambled over, and clinging lianas confronted us at every turn. We were altogether too large, too bulky, and too clumsy for this sort of expedition.

At one point we came to a dirt road, and my spirits soared. But Chico hustled us across it. "Too hot on the road," he advised. "It's much easier cutting through the forest." Half an hour later the path crossed a patch of scrubby cleared land, and somewhere I could hear the sound of cattle. "That's the ranch," he explained. "There's a few peons living in there. They don't bother us much. But the rancher is talking about doing some logging, and that could lead to a lot of trouble."

The path took us into the forest once more, until finally we came upon the clearing where Dona Rosane's family lived. Their house was set up above a bend in the muddy river. They had re-cently planted maize and manioc; mango trees, pupunha palms, sugar cane, and bananas were growing round the house.

The family all turned out to welcome us. "This is my husband, Hélio," said Dona Rosane, "and this is my daughter Jacira and her husband. This one here is my smallest grandchild. Isn't she a sweetie?" She beamed. Chico's wife and three blonde little girls were sitting on the front veranda; the youngest child scuffled about in the dust outside, together with an assortment of ducks, chickens, and small pigs.

The place of honor inside belonged to an ancient treadle sewing machine. In the kitchen, a wood stove was covered with an assortment of simmering pots, and a washing-up basin sat on a platform outside so that the water could drain out underneath. In one corner stood a small hand grinder; next to it a big basket of corn waited to be ground. The one bedroom contained a large bed draped with a pink net; clothes hung neatly across a few bamboos. On top of a chest of drawers were family photos and lots of little bottles of pills.

We were taken into the kitchen for the ritual cup of sweet black coffee. This house had no water filter, and the water—from a covered jar—looked muddy. We managed a surreptitious swig from our water bottle, and then went out to join Hélio on the front veranda.

"I've been on this holding for ten years now," he told us. "Before that we were over in the Purus valley. But this is a good place for rubber, particularly the other side of the river. That's Bolivia over there, did you know?

"We've got about 990 acres here. But the rubber trees on this side aren't in very good shape. You have to treat them well, you know, otherwise they get exhausted. We've got five rubber trails, and three of us working here: my son Chico, myself, and Joãozinho—he works here as a sharecropper. Do you see that building over there? That's the rubber house. We used to smoke the rubber in there, but these days we use vinegar and put it in a press. Much less work, although I don't think, myself, that you get the same quality.

"Of course you have to have a way with the rubber trees. Otherwise they just won't work for you. You've probably seen how we tap the rubber? We'll take you out tomorrow and show you. You can try for yourself, if you like.

"Did you meet Senhor Birroque? He's the boss. We've always got on well together, he and I. He sends a mule train in to collect the rubber, and it brings our supplies at the same time. He knows a lot about medicine too; he holds a clinic out at the trading post on Sundays, and he can do anything just as well as the doctors—stitch up cuts, set bones, and pull out teeth. And he'll always let us have whatever medicines we need. Doesn't even charge us, half the time."

"Well, however nice he may be, we'd still be better off without him," put in Chico, who had been listening attentively. "If we didn't have a boss, then we wouldn't have to pay rent, and we'd be able to sell our rubber through a cooperative like they do in Xapuri. They get better prices than we do, and they buy their supplies more cheaply. I mean, we don't seem to get much change at the end of the day on this seringal. There's always more owing than coming in, it seems to me."

Later in the afternoon we went down to bathe in the muddy river. Dona Rosane outfitted us in T-shirts, and we splashed happily away. "Hope there aren't any *candirus*," said Juliet, laughing. *Candirus* are nasty little fishes that swim up into human orifices and attach themselves with a barb. They cause excruciating pain and have to be surgically removed.

"*Candirus*?" said Dona Rosane, "why yes, we do have them here." Clutching ourselves, we sprinted for the bank.

Supper was held by lamplight. We helped ourselves out of pots brimming with chicken, manioc flour, spaghetti, and rice. We had been feeding the smallest member of the family on biscuits all along, and by this time she had figured out where they were kept and was hanging around like a hopeful puppy. A pet agouti (a small furry animal) came in to collect his evening snack and neatly gnawed on a chicken bone. The conversation wound gently on as we ate, and shortly afterwards everyone took to their hammocks. All night long the pigs rooted and grunted under the house, uttering occasional snorts and squeaks of protest. At three o'clock the cock started to crow. The entire household was on its feet well before dawn.

"Dona, oh Dona!" Outside the window I could barely make out the shape of Joãozinho, come to take us on the rubber trail. "Bring your camera," he begged, "I want you to take my picture." He marched off toward the river and walked easily across a narrow, wobbly log. Juliet and I looked at each other and tried to summon up our courage. Joãozinho instantly sized up the situation. "Take a pole to lean on," he advised, with a sly grin. We hobbled across, leaning heavily on the pole, which kept getting itself stuck in the glutinous mud and was more of a hindrance than a help.

Joãozinho placed a notched stick against a rubber tree and climbed nimbly up, bare toes curling around the wood. "You make a diagonal cut like this," he explained, "and then you place the cup at the bottom to catch the latex. There are 172 trees on this path, and it'll take me about three hours to go around. Then I come back in the afternoon and collect the latex. Chico and I will process it this evening. We use vinegar these days, which makes it much quicker than it used to be. Take my picture please." He posed at the top, brandishing his knife, while we clicked away in the dim light, taking pictures that would never come out.

"I'm working here with Hélio and Chico," he continued. "The place belongs to Hélio, and I'm a sharecropper. He can't work at present because he's been sick, so Chico and I are doing it all. Mind you, we'll have to stop when the rains really set in. This area will be flooded, and anyway you can't tap rubber in the rain. So we'll move to the other side and concentrate on collecting the Brazil nuts. Well, if you'll excuse me, I must be off. Don't forget to put me in your book." He hopped down the tree and went on his way, whistling.

Back at the house we were given large bowls of chicken and rice. It was not yet seven o'clock. "I'm going over to one of the neighbors," said Dona Rosane. "I'll set you on your way, if you like."

An hour's walk brought us to Maria's house. She was pounding rice with a friend who had popped in to give her a hand. Maria is one of the few female rubber tappers. "I do everything around this place," she said cheerfully, belaboring the rice. "You can't rely on men to get things done properly. Of course, I'm as strong as a man. They don't call me Big Blackie for nothing.

"My first husband, he and I came up from Espírito Santo together and went to Pimenta Bueno over in Rondônia to cut rubber. My mother told me that man was no good, but of course I didn't listen. How right she was! See this scar on my leg? That's where I got bitten by a snake. Almost lost the leg. I had to spend five months in the hospital in Porto Velho. When I came out, I found that my husband had fixed himself up with another woman. He expected me to sleep right in the same bed with them both, can you imagine? Well, I didn't stand for *that*. I kicked him out and I came on up to Acre. I heard it was a good place for rubber, and I'd got used to the life.

"Then I got myself another man, but he wasn't any better than the first. It wasn't long before he started messing around with some woman, and then she walked out on him and left her baby behind. And he came to me and asked me to look after it! I was so mad, I couldn't decide whether to shoot him or the child or both of them. In the end I kept the child. It wasn't her fault nobody wanted her. But I told him to clear out and never come back again.

"I've got another fellow now. Third time lucky maybe? And

I'm pregnant again. I'm hoping for a boy this time. I've got ten girls already."

Maria's friend, Neni, was determined that we should visit her house as well. We waved good-bye to the dauntless Maria and set off once more through the forest.

Neni lived in the smallest house imaginable. Its one room was entirely taken up by a big bed where the whole family slept— eight of them. At the bed's foot stood a small charcoal cooker and a water filter. Plates, cups, spoons, clothes, a radio, a machete, and a shotgun hung neatly on the wall.

She blew expertly on the charcoal, producing coffee in a few moments. "This is my youngest," she said proudly, taking the child from a slightly larger sibling. "He's had a lot of sickness, poor little soul. It's left him really weak. He doesn't walk yet, although he's two years old. Senhor Birroque has sent me this new medicine to try. I think he's getting a bit stronger. What do you think?"

Clearly all was not well with the child. He could hardly hold his head up. It would take more than a bottle of medicine to solve his problem.

We heard a jingling of harness outside and the mule train trotted briskly up; it had come to load up the rubber. It was accompanied by a cheerful mule driver and the local malaria control officer. The latter was an unabashed city man dressed in a tight uniform with dark glasses and a packet of "Charm" cigarettes. He did know his stuff, however, and visited the rubber tappers regularly. He questioned Neni closely about each of the children. One of them had been suffering from recurring fevers, so the health officer whipped out a needle and made a blood slide on the spot.

"I look after 633 families on this *seringal*," he told us. "I try to come around every couple of months or so—more often in the wet season, because there's more malaria then. And we're on the alert for cholera too. It hasn't surfaced yet in this area, but we're keeping a sharp eye out for it.

"There's a generally low level of health among the rubber tappers," he confided, when our hostess went off to get more coffee. "That smallest child, for example. I'm afraid he's going to be severely retarded. Dona Neni had a difficult birth, but of course she doesn't know that's the reason. And Dona Rosane's place, that's one of the main centers of malaria around here. If you start getting fevers, check in with one of our people.

"Another thing is the sanitation. These people haven't much idea, and of course the children are full of parasites. Some of them drink water straight out of the river, so it's not surprising."

After coffee, all of us trooped over to another much larger house. About twelve people, including the muleteer, were having lunch—an unappetizing mixture of gristly meat and gravelly manioc flour. Another malaria patient in this family stoically held out his finger to be pricked, then swallowed the bitter chloroquine without protest.

"I'm going back to Birroque's," said the muleteer. "You can come with me if you like. I think we should be leaving now. There's a storm coming up." Gratefully, we put the pack on one of the donkeys and headed off through the forest. "It's about four hours from here," added the boy. More like six for us, I thought to myself.

Back in the dense forest, I hoped that the storm, when it did come, wouldn't soak us to the skin. Wrong again. Within minutes the sky darkened and the rain attacked us maliciously. The trail became a rushing torrent; each of us trudged along locked in private misery. Water streamed off our faces so that we could hardly see where we were going as we sloshed through ankle-deep mud and occasionally fell into large holes. I clutched the camera to me. Even though it was wrapped in layers of plastic, it seemed impossible that it could stay dry. At one point the muleteer took pity on Juliet, who was limping because of blisters, and lent her his horse. Five minutes later horse and rider fell off a slippery bridge into the muddy waters beneath.

Late that afternoon we squelched into the trading post, stinking, wet, and miserable. The woman of the house swept us inside to change our filthy clothes and drink gallons of hot coffee. The bunkhouse was large and friendly, with rows of lumpy beds, a long table, and a huge ancient stove covered with blackened pots. We would have gladly settled in for the night, but we needed to get back to town. Cleaner and drier, but still smelling powerfully of wet donkey, we boarded the bus. The other passengers scattered as we approached.

Back in Rio Branco we made our way to the Casa do Seringueiro in the main square. It houses a small Rubber Tappers' Museum whose friendly staff was happy to fill us in on the rubber trade. We talked to Amina, a historian from the state university who is making a series of videos about rubber and rubber tappers.

"It's a fascinating story, the story of rubber," she began. "The Indians were the ones who discovered how to use it. They made torches out of it, and waterproof bags and bottles. Eventually the technique reached Belém in Pará, and by the end of the eighteenth century they were sending all sorts of rubber products to Europe and New England.

"But there was one problem. The rubber may have been waterproof, but it wasn't weatherproof. In the heat it went sticky, and in the cold it went hard and brittle. It took nearly a hundred years before someone discovered how to process it properly. After that, the demand was suddenly huge. Rubber was used to make shoes, belts, braces, bags, and tires for bicycles and later for cars. People couldn't get enough of it. And it all came from the Amazon.

"Well, you've been to the *seringal,* and you saw how the trees grow—scattered throughout the forest. So it's never been easy stuff to harvest. In the early days people used to paddle out along the rivers and tap the trees as they found them. They figure that by 1875 there were up to 25,000 tappers working out of Belém! The more enterprising ones laid claim to large areas of forest and began employing other people to do the work for them, thereby leaving themselves free to sell the rubber in the city.

"Demand grew steadily, and traders started to look for other areas to exploit. They traveled all over the Amazon region, and they found that the richest rubber area of all was here in Acre. But there wasn't anyone living here to harvest it for them. At that point they had a stroke of luck. There was a terrible drought over in Ceará, in the northeast, and thousands of people fled to the cities. So the rubber traders went in and signed up men as fast as they could. They offered to pay their fares and give them all the equipment they would need: guns, knives, machetes, food, and clothes. What the men didn't realize was that they would have to pay off the debt in rubber, and they'd never clear it as long as they lived. They couldn't read or write, you see, so they were completely at the mercy of the bosses.

The Cearenses had a pretty rough time. They couldn't take the climate and kept getting sick and dying. The bosses were always short of men. They used to send gangs in to hunt down the Indians and force them into the labor pool. Most of *them* died, either of bad treatment or of white man's diseases. They had no immunity, you see. We estimate that seventy whole tribes were wiped out during that time, and of course all their lands were taken over by the rubber bosses.

"So you had this extraordinary situation. There were the rubber tappers stuck in the forest. They couldn't afford to send for their families, so they had to take local women instead. They weren't even allowed to grow any food. So they collected rubber and Brazil nuts, and they did a bit of hunting and a bit of fishing, and they never did pay off their debts. Meanwhile the bosses were living in incredible luxury in Manaus and Belém, drinking champagne and going to the opera.

"Then the whole thing crashed. You remember that the British had set up rubber plantations in Malaya, using seed smuggled from the Amazon? Well, when that rubber hit the world markets, the bottom fell out of the Amazon rubber trade. The bosses went bust, and moved out. The *seringueiros* kept going somehow, and they sold their rubber to the few remaining boat traders. In one generation the population of this state declined by twenty percent. The place practically closed down.

"But amazingly enough there came another boom. It was during the Second World War. The Malayan plantations had fallen into the hands of the Japanese, and the Americans were suddenly desperate for rubber. They said they wanted 100,000 tons! Just to give you an idea, the whole of Amazônia produces 30,000 tons a year at present.

"Anyway, the Americans made a deal with the Brazilian government to buy as much rubber as could be produced. So the government people went back to the northeast to recruit rubber tappers. They called it the Rubber Army and set the whole thing up on a patriotic footing. They promised them the moon, too: free uniforms, free passages, medical benefits, repatriation, military pensions, the lot.

"Once the recruits got to the Amazon, they were in exactly the same situation as their predecessors. When the war finally ended, they never saw hide nor hair of their pensions. In fact, it's only now, forty-five years later, that the government is starting to pay up. How many rubber soldiers do you suppose are still alive?

"Well, after the war was won, the whole thing slumped again. The Amazon simply couldn't compete. Henry Ford had tried twice to grow rubber in plantations, but it couldn't be done—not in the Amazon. So the trade gradually faded out. In the 1960s the government withdrew the rubber subsidies, and finally the Rubber Bank failed.

"Most of the remaining bosses pushed off, but the rubber tappers, of course, were still around. They didn't have to pay rents anymore, but that didn't stop their exploitation—this time by the traders.

"Since there was practically nothing happening in Acre, the governor thought that he'd better do something about the situation. So he invited a whole lot of businessmen from the south to come in and set up cattle ranches. He had this dream about the road to the Pacific, and how Acre would become rich and famous. He as much as gave the land away, and naturally the ranchers started chopping the forest down. People had to leave. Fifteen thousand *seringueiro* families moved to Bolivia, and they're still there. At least another 5,000 families had to get out; most of them ended up in the cities. It was then that the tappers started organizing themselves. You'll be going to Xapuri, and you can talk to them there, but there's someone here you might be interested to meet. His name is Maurício, and he's quite an activist in his way."

Maurício had been in town to attend a meeting of leaders of the base communities of the church. We asked him just what a base community was.

"A base community? It's a local church group. We meet for worship and instruction, and we talk about social issues. For instance, in our community we're looking at the whole business of social justice. We're thinking about ways in which we could change the system in order to bring about a fairer society. We're encouraging people to join the union and take an active part in pressing for change here and now. It's a very practical form of Christianity, you might say. We're not waiting for things to get better when we get to heaven. We're looking for things to get better here and now.

"Speaking of justice, my father was a case in point. He came from Ceará as one of the rubber soldiers. They were supposed to be given salaries and pensions and all that, but my father died without ever receiving a penny.

"I was born on the *seringal* and started tapping rubber when I was about nine or ten. We had a large family, sixteen of us altogether, although two of my sisters died when they were babies. I was the eldest boy in the family, and when I got big enough my father would take me with him when he went off in the morning. He used to say that you had to have the right touch for the rubber trees, otherwise you would never get them to work for you. He showed me how to make the cuts on the bark, just so. If you cut too deep, you hurt the tree and you might even kill it, he told me.

"We used to get up so early it would still be dark. My father would give me a lump of brown sugar sometimes, and we would take a handful of flour to eat. I was always hungry, I remember that! I suppose that all children are. My father used to take a *poronga* with him. I don't know whether you've seen one of those? It's a little lamp you wear on your head. I remember following the light through the forest, although my father didn't actually use it often. He could see anything. If you walk a lot in the dark, you don't need a light.

"We'd walk around the trail and make the cuts in the trees, and he'd show me just where to put the cup to catch the latex when it started to bleed. I remember thinking that it was the nicest time of day. It still is my favorite time, just around dawn when the whole forest is starting to wake up.

"My father always carried a gun, of course. Sometimes he would shoot something to take back for lunch: paca [a large rodent] or armadillo, or occasionally a big bird. We'd be through by mid-morning, and then we'd have something to eat, usually *farinha*—that's manioc flour—sometimes with a little meat if my father had shot anything, or some fish. Later in the day we'd go off again and collect the latex. We'd bring it back and build a fire and smoke it. It used to smell dreadful, and the smoke would make us cough. People don't do it that way anymore, thank goodness.

"When the boat came, we'd trade the rubber for supplies. In the old days they used to sell to the bosses, but most of them had left by that time, so we used to trade with the merchants. We didn't have to pay rent, but we never seemed to make any money either. It was because the merchants were cheating us—almost as bad as the bosses, really.

"The trading post was about three hours' walk from our place, and the rubber was awkward stuff to carry. My father would take in about 80 pounds at a time. I always enjoyed going with him. We'd stack all the rubber up and weigh it out, and then the merchant would write down in his little book just how much we'd brought in and give us our supplies: sugar, flour, oil, ammunition, kerosene. We always thought they were robbing us, but we couldn't ever prove it. We couldn't read or write, you see, because there weren't any schools. We have a school now, though. Very good it is. My children go there, and my eldest boy, he's eight, he can read and write his name already.

"I started working regularly with my father when I was about ten. I was big for my age, so it was easy for me, and I remember feeling very grown-up. Around that time the ranchers started coming up from the south. They'd buy the land and cut down the forest, and then there'd be all sorts of trouble. We *seringueiros* had been there for generations, you see, but we didn't have any titles. There was something called 'squatters' rights,' which meant that you could claim the land if you'd been working on it. But your rights weren't worth much when the ranchers sent their gunmen after you! Most of us hadn't ever heard of squatters' rights anyway.

"We had a radio in our house, and I remember hearing when the trouble started in this area. The ranchers used to send their *pistoleiros* in. Well, you can't argue with *pistoleiros*, can you? So people had to leave. If they didn't, they might get their houses burnt down. Then they'd have to go. Some of them would go to the towns, where it wasn't easy for them. At least in the forest you could get wood to cook with, and you could catch a fish, and keep a cow or a pig. Not in the town. They didn't have anywhere to live, and no money. It must have been terrible.

"Later on the union started up. My father wasn't keen on that sort of thing. He said that he didn't want to get involved with politics and the police. Better to stay in the forest and keep out of trouble, he used to say. But I was interested in learning more about it, and one day I went off to the town to find out for myself. They said that things were changing fast, and that we rubber tappers needed to learn to read and write so that we could manage our own affairs and not be at the mercy of the traders. I could see that that made sense.

"Sometime after that a priest came out to the *seringal* and talked to us about base communities. He said that it wasn't right that we should be cheated by the traders or evicted by the ranchers, and that if we worked together we could get a fair deal. He told us that Jesus came to free us from exploitation and that we should rise up and fight for our rights. So I got involved from the very beginning, and we started organizing our community. We've already got a school, and we're hoping to get a health post next.

"Then some of the *seringueiros* from Xapuri went down to Brasília and started up the National Council of Rubber Tappers. Imagine that, getting into a bus and traveling all that way just to start up our own union! Well, they found out that nobody in the government was interested in us and our doings, and it didn't matter to them if the ranchers came in and chopped down all the forest. So we realized that if we wanted to stop the ranchers, we'd have to do it ourselves.

"People started getting shot then. I remember the night we heard that Chico Mendes had died. A wonderful man, Chico. He was a real inspiration to us all. And look what we've achieved. We've got some schools already, and health posts, although the government says that it hasn't got any money, so we have to pay the monitors ourselves out of the money we have in our co-op. Now that's one thing that *is* working well. We're getting much better prices these days. We even have a cash surplus at the end of the year. Not that money's worth much, is it? And now we're getting these extractive reserves. That means that the land will be safe from the ranchers. It'll belong to our union, and we'll all have thirty-year leases on it.

"There are things we still have to sort out. I mean, we'd like to be able to leave our holdings to our sons, and be able to sell them or swap them if we want to move. We don't spend all our lives in the same spot—not in this part of the state anyway. Over on the Juruá River, some of the *seringueiros* still live in the old way. Captive rubber tappers, they call them. That means they pay rent to the bosses like our fathers did. But now they're starting to organize the unions over there too. At least they don't have all this trouble with the ranchers.

"As for the ranchers, they're only clearing the land because they want to sell it again at a good profit. Do you think they really care about cattle? Not them. That's the sin of it, don't you see? There they go, cutting the forest, and the rubber tappers and the river people who have always lived there have to clear out, and what for? So the ranchers can sell the land for a tidy sum when they build the new road. Well, I hope it never happens.

"One more thing. The price of rubber is down. Did you know that you can't even buy a pound of sugar for a pound of rubber with what they're paying these days? Well, some of our people went down to Brasília again just last month to talk to the president about it. They said that we couldn't live with the price so low. Do you know what? They got the price up 300 percent. That's what people working together can do.

"Mind you, we'll have to find other things to market out of the forest now that they've got rubber plantations down in the south. But there are several possibilities—nuts, for instance. It's very rich around here for nuts, and fruits, and oils and essences too. There's a lot of things we could be selling from our forest, if only they'll give us half a chance."

Juliet and I settled down in the bar in Rio Branco and tried to make something of what the *seringueiros* had told us.

It's not as if they are making a decent living. They are using extremely primitive technology and producing a poor-quality product, and still they live in poverty. Now that the rubber plantations in São Paulo are about to begin production, can there be any future for the Amazon rubber tappers? Aren't they an anachronism, perhaps standing in the way of progress, as the ranchers maintain?

They complain that they have no access to proper education and health facilities, but does it make economic sense to provide all that for just a handful of people? And as for the uproar when Chico Mendes was murdered: What was so special about him? People get murdered all the time.

Could the extractive reserves provide the answer? Are they really something that could work, or just another crazy Amazon idea?

We asked Osmar, the union leader from Xapuri, what he thought.

"What is all the fuss about? It's about justice, that's what it's about. Chico was the first to understand what was happening when those ranchers started coming in and cutting our forest. He told us the government wasn't going to lift a finger to help us. He said that it was up to us to stop the ranchers before they burnt the whole place down around our ears. He told us we'd better learn how to read so that we could look out for ourselves, and he showed us that if we got together we could change things.

"And we have. It's slow, but it's happening. We've got our own National Council now. We've managed to get the government to set up some extractive reserves. We need a lot more, but it's a start. It means that the forests will be preserved, and that we'll be able to go on living as we always have.

"People are starting to think about how we could be using other forest products as well—*cupuaçu* fruit, for example. It makes the best ice cream. Have you tried it? There are oils too, and medicinal plants. And we could be planting things like cocoa, and *guaraná*, and even rubber.

"The cooperative is going well, down in Xapuri. There's an American company that's buying our Brazil nuts directly from us and paying us a decent price at last. We're hoping to set up more cooperatives. And we've got our literacy programs and our health posts.

"We've made an alliance with the Indians too. That's pretty remarkable! Indians and *seringueiros* have been enemies for years, but now we're pledged to work together on things that concern us all as People of the Forest.

"The point is this. People are starting to realize that it doesn't make sense to go on destroying the forest. And we *seringueiros* have been living here for years without damaging it. There are studies that show that you can make more money out of the standing forest than you can by clearing it. By improving the conditions of the forest people you'll be ensuring the survival of the forest, and everyone will be happy.

"One of the things that happened when Chico died was that people all over the world got to hear about us and our struggle. You be sure to tell them about us, in that book of yours. Tell them that we're working away in the forest here, and we need all the help we can get. Tell them to support forest products, and to go on pressing for social justice. And tell them not to forget us."

10

IDEALISTS

Defend the fatherless, do justice to the needy.
Deliver the poor and needy; rid them out of the
hand of the wicked.

—Psalm 82

"Liberation theology? It's just taking what Jesus said literally, that's all." In Rio Branco, Padre Pedro Paulo sipped his beer meditatively. "The Messiah came to set the captives free, didn't he? The Old Testament talks of 'justice rolling like a river.' Don't think of Jesus as being meek and mild. He was a revolutionary. If you look at the Gospel, it's dynamite.

"The church in Latin America has traditionally been on the side of the status quo—in other words, the big landowners and the government. It was in the 1960s that liberation theology first emerged. Those were dark days in Latin America. There had been a wave of military takeovers, and human rights were being violated on every side. Of all moments in history, that was when the church chose to stand up for the poor and oppressed!

"There was a lot of opposition, as you may suppose, both from within the church and from outside. We were accused of being communists, of course, but we stuck to our guns. After all, the Gospel never says that we have to put up with injustice here on earth. The kingdom of heaven is supposed to start here and now, and it's up to God's people to make sure that it happens. That means we've got to fight for justice and righteousness.

"We started off by founding the base communities. They were to be focal points for prayer and discussion. Don't forget that in those days people weren't allowed to meet together, except in church. Well, part of our work of consciousness-raising involved encouraging people to set up associations and unions so that they'd have a base for action.

"In 1973 Dom Moacyr came up to be the bishop of Acre Purus. He's a wonderful man, a mover and shaker. Nobody in those days had any political experience, you see. We had to start from the beginning. We used to discuss human rights, trying to help people understand the issues facing them and think about ways of tackling them. But we didn't just talk about things, we made sure we actually did something; we helped organize sit-ins, or strikes, or land invasions. At that point we began to run into more and more antagonism—chiefly from the landowners, but also from the police. We started getting death threats, so we knew we must be doing something right!

"As the government began to open up a bit we began consolidating our position. Our people from the Indigenous Missionary Council and the Pro-Indian Commission were working to support the Indians, and the Pastoral Lands Commission was involved in all questions relating to land disputes. It's important to document everything carefully. We keep complete records of everything that's going on.

"In the 1980s we came out increasingly strongly in defense of the workers. The more we stood up for them, the more we put ourselves in the firing line. The Council of Bishops backed us to the hilt, even though that led to considerable problems with the Vatican. We began to see that we had to defend the earth itself, not just the children of the earth. We realized that the kind of predatory development that was going on was causing irreparable harm to the rivers and the forests and to the very air we breathe. We saw that when people lost their lands, they lost their livelihoods and sometimes even their lives.

"Well, this sort of thinking doesn't endear us to the people who are making money out of logging and mining, and the government doesn't like it when we accuse it of committing genocide against the Indians. So we haven't many friends in high places—except One!"

Next we talked to the bishop, Dom Moacyr Grecchi. In his sixties, greying, with glasses, he has the look of someone who thinks deeply—the look of a man of God.

"I have been in this diocese for nearly twenty years. When I came, the stampede for land was just beginning. Land was incredibly cheap. Everyone began to grab as much as he could. The connivance of the authorities extended from the lowliest government employee right up to the Justice Department. Everything was for sale. Everyone was bribed. It was a cruel time.

"Then the landowners started forcing the *seringueiros* out. Around here, they used to get the police to do their dirty work for them. One day the rubber tappers would look out the window and there would be a large group of uniformed policemen standing outside. Well, that was enough for them. They couldn't afford a fight. Usually they fled, leaving behind everything they owned. Nobody did anything for them. Hardly anyone even knew about it. The press was censored.

"So we started to do what we could. Ironically, we were helped a lot by INCRA, the land settlement agency. We printed up a lot of posters quoting the laws. The tappers couldn't read, of course, but they began to understand that there was a law to support them. The main barrier was their ignorance. They were all stuck out there in their forests, and they didn't really know what was going on.

"The man who set up the unions was João Maia. He'd been sent up from Brasília to get them going. Then union members started taking direct action. They'd denounce someone for cutting the forest without permission, or they'd have a sit-in, or they'd have a demonstration. They usually got beaten up by the police, of course, but we gave them all the encouragement we could.

"I don't think the government took us seriously. I remember the night when the governor told me that the people of Acre weren't ready for unions. The very next day we had a big meeting here in the cathedral; as a result of that meeting, the first union was set up—right here in this cathedral. Chico Mendes was very active in all that. As the dictatorship eased up a bit, we began to get some publicity. We were mentioned a few times in the papers and on the radio.

"It wasn't ever clear sailing, and it still isn't. The conservative wing of the church doesn't like us at all, and neither does the state government. The right-wing politicians do their best to corrupt the union leaders, and I'm sorry to say that they succeed more often than not. People are easily bought."

Anselmo is the local representative of the Indigenous Missionary Council. He works in a small cramped office in the parish house, and he is always shouting into the phone at someone on the other side of the state, or delving into his files, or dictating memos about the state of the Indians.

"How are things with the Indians? Bad, very bad. It's the land question. Although lots of areas technically belong to them, hardly any of the lands have been officially demarcated, let alone protected, and they're wide open to any logger or gold miner or squatter that wants to go in. Let me tell you about the case of the Mequens in Rondônia. Their lands are under dispute. A few months ago, one of the local *deputados* sent squatters into the area and paid them to start cutting the forest. He told them that the place was going to be made into a new township, and that he was going to be the mayor. Well, the chief of the Mequens came to us. We had to get the federal police to intervene because the local police wouldn't touch it. Now the squatters are camped out on the *deputado*'s farm, and he's pretty mad!

"The loggers are just as bad. The big boys send in the small loggers, and when we do manage to summon the police, somebody always tips them off before the police arrive. Cat and mouse stuff all the time. Still, it keeps them on their toes. It seems to me that I'm always running around putting out fires, and I never have a chance to do anything constructive.

"Government policy on the Indians? Well, when Collor first came in, he went in for Rambo gestures, like dynamiting the *garimpeiros'* airstrips up in the Yanomami area. It was purely cosmetic, as everyone said at the time. The *garimpeiros* are all back there working away harder than ever. On the other hand, the government *has* finally got around to demarcating the reserves for the Yanomami and the Kayapó. Well, that's great. It was probably in response to international pressures and not for the right reasons at all. But I don't care why they did it as long as it got done. Day-to-day stuff, now that's a different matter. They haven't given any money to FUNAI [the Federal Indian Authority]. It's practically bankrupt. I think it's part of a deliberate policy of theirs to run it down. Of course the Indians are completely dependent on FUNAI, so they're in worse straits than they were before.

"Everything that is happening up here at the moment is the focus of international attention. You must have been following all this fuss about the internationalization of the Amazon? It's an interesting case. It's military thinking, you see. The whole development of Amazônia was brought about on the initiative of the generals, back in the 1970s. There were two reasons that they gave. One was that they wanted to secure the frontier regions against foreigners who might covet our mineral resources. They were particularly concerned about migrant tribes like the Yanomami who move across international borders. They thought they might get subverted, I suppose! The second reason was so that Brazil could become a superpower. Let me show you a quote from a top-secret military document about the future of Amazônia. It was published in September 1989. Here's what it says: 'In this document we place our faith and hope that those who lead our nation through this period [1990s] illuminated by God, and acting for the greater good of our people, will be able to act with resolution and courage. . . . We firmly believe that, as the nineteenth century belonged to Great Britain, and the twentieth century to the United States of America, so the twenty-first century will belong to that great nation of the tropics: Brazil.'

"As you know, soldiers have to have an enemy. In the old days they could point to the communists and say that they were the enemy, although there was never much support for them in Brazil. Still, they did provide a target. Then they faded away, and now the military has to find another scapegoat. If you can mobilize national opinion against some enemy—preferably an outsider—you can divert attention from the fact that things aren't going too well internally. So now they've got a new enemy: the foreigners and the eco-imperialists, whoever they are. Mind you, when senators from North America go about referring to Amazônia as the legacy of mankind, and the president of France calls it an international patrimony, they're setting themselves up for that sort of thing.

"But look what happens next. Anyone within Brazil who criticizes the government's development plans is automatically classified as being in league with the enemy. Because some of the environmentalist NGOs [nongovernmental organizations] get international funding, the government assumes that we're all in the conspiracy. They've got it into their heads that there's a North American plot to tie up huge areas of Amazônia, supposedly for ecological purposes, but actually so that they can seize control of our mineral resources someday. The irony is that this xenophobia appeals not only to the right-wing military, but also to the left-wing radicals. So we're getting flak from both sides.

"The whole thing is a red herring anyway. There has always been international involvement in Amazônia, right from the beginning. The rubber trade was mostly in the hands of the British and the Americans. Most of the mining companies are multinationals, and both mining and logging depend on international markets. All the Great Projects—the roads and dams and settlement schemes—were funded internationally. There are even foreign missionaries working with the Indians. So the whole place has already been internationalized!"

Anselmo sent us over to the Worker's Council of Amazônia. "Those guys are working on the nitty-gritty stuff of workers' legislation," he said. "It's not very romantic, but it has to be done."

Theirs was another tiny office, this one so crammed with files that there was no space to sit down.

"Sorry about all this stuff," said Rubinho, the boss. "I can't put it away because there's nowhere to put it. Just a minute, let's at least put on the fan." Triumphantly he produced a small creaking fan that was unable to cope with the oppressive heat of the afternoon.

"I suppose it was Anselmo who sent you over to see me? Well, what can I do for you? You want to know about the extractive reserves? We're working on the legal side, together with the National Council of Seringueiros. Let me tell you how far we've got.

"The first thing, after identifying the area, is to get the land expropriated. The ownership is then conceded to an association of *seringueiros*. It's a collective title. The exact terms under which the association will operate are to be defined later. There are lots of points to be sorted out. The leases will probably run for thirty years, with provision made for them to sell their holdings to another *seringueiro*. They tend to move around quite a lot, so we have to make allowances for that. Fishing and hunting rights will be held in common, although the rubber trails will be privately leased, and the leaseholder will have all extractive rights to his lands. The *seringueiros* won't pay rent, but they will pay something toward the cooperative. That money will go for schools and health posts and infrastructure in general.

"Sometimes they don't want to join the co-op, and that's something we're going to have to work on. The thing is, they're used to the system they've got, and they can't see any reason to change it. They've built up a relationship with the traders over the years, and often the traders advance them goods against their rubber crops. They're not really accustomed to dealing in money, and if they pay it out to the co-op, they may not see any immediate returns—nothing concrete like the rifle that the traders might advance them.

"But they're slowly getting used to working with one another. There are different groupings: the base community, the co-op, the union, sometimes they have a football team. And things like taking part in *empates* (that's what they call their sit-ins) generate a certain community spirit. They already have a kind of extended family tradition, swapping labor and giving one another a hand when they need it. The teachers in the school, for instance, are unpaid members of the community. Other families help out their families in exchange. And they make their own curriculum in the school. That way they can feel that it's really theirs."

Our next stop was the National Council of Rubber Tappers. We talked to Armando, who is a data processor for it as well as for other like-minded organizations. Dark, bearded, intense, he wears Indian jewelry and punctuates his conversation with frequent hand gestures.

"I got to Acre in the early 1980s. It was a grand time then for people who wanted to get something done. I managed to land a job in FUNAI. It was financially solvent in those days, and relatively open-minded. I worked with the Kaxinawá down on the Rio Breu. It was great. But it didn't last. A few years later FUNAI had one of its periodic purges and I was fired, along with ninety-something of my colleagues.

"Then I worked on the Projeto Seringueiro, together with Fátima, my wife. We lived on the *seringal*. Fátima worked in the school, and I was on the health side. It really gave us an idea of the problems they face.

"But one of the things that struck us was that they're so very conservative—narrow-minded, really. They're only now, reluctantly, beginning to realize that their interests are the same as those of the Indians, and that they'd better work together if they want to change things. And they still can't find any common ground with the settlers, which is a pity. They're going to have to open their minds a bit and start thinking about the future, otherwise they're just going to fade away.

"I worked with the settlers too for a while, just when they were starting to come in. I had a job with INCRA [the Land Settlement Board]. You'd see the colonists arriving from Paraná or somewhere. Sometimes they were still speaking their own brands of German or whatever, and they were just dumped in the forest and left to get on with it. Of course they'd try to do things in the way they knew. And usually they failed. Some people say that Acre could be a big agricultural state. I don't believe that. The soils are poor. Whatever happens, we've got to make sure that this place is kept under forest."

To see what was happening on the save-the-forest front, we called in at the State Environmental Institute to talk to the ecologists. In the lobby we met Alba, one of the biologists.

"Give me a beer and I'll tell you anything you want to hear," she said mischievously. We decamped to the nearest bar and she began.

"Why am I here? Well that's a good question. I sometimes ask myself why I'm here." She ran her hand through her curly blonde hair and grinned. "I'd say I'm here because I want to be where it's at. I'm one of those crazy people who believes that if you want something to be done, you'd better go out and do it. And I'm here to make sure that they don't cut down every last tree in the Amazon.

"I think that people like me come for all sorts of reasons. Some of us have a purely scientific interest—researchers or Ph.D. students who want to do something wonderful that hasn't been done before, like finding the cure for AIDS or documenting some special kind of beetle. Then there are the do-gooders. They're here to work for human rights, or because they have some screwed-up idea of how to save the Indians. Then there are the simple lifers, the hopeless romantics, and even the guilt-ridden rich kids. But all of us are here basically to fight for the forest and for the people of the forest. That puts us in the opposite camp from people who are cutting it down and moving the people out—the big projects like ranching, hydropower, and settlement schemes. Sure, we think that the mining and the logging industries should be much more rigidly controlled. But it's not as if we're some bunch of weirdos that is opposed to any form of development. Not at all. We've got to make sure it's done in a way that doesn't ruin the whole place, that's all.

"You may have noticed that there's a bit of a gap between the Amazônians and the rest of us. They're very protective of their turf—it's not surprising really—and when people like me come up here we have to watch our step to start with. I think they're fed up with all these outsiders telling them what they should be doing all the time, and that's understandable. So if you detect a bit of resentment from time to time, it isn't because you're *gringos*. It's because you're not Amazônians.

"I remember I was at the university one day, and I suddenly felt that I couldn't face writing one more paper about the problems of the Amazon while I was sitting there in Rio de Janeiro. I might as well have been writing about Siberia. So I decided not to write another word until I'd been here, and lived here, and worked here, and knew what I was talking about. Makes sense, doesn't it?

"I suppose, if you had to classify us, and I *hate* doing that, you could say that we are well-educated, middle-class people with a social conscience. And look what we've got ourselves mixed up in! We may have thought we were saving the forest, but we didn't necessarily expect to find ourselves involved in all these hot issues, like land wars and murder! I mean, we're just a bunch of biologists, and zoologists, and anthropologists, and lawyers, and sociologists. And we're in this thing up to our necks. Most of us are branded as left-wing troublemakers. We're not exactly risking our lives, but we're certainly risking our jobs, particularly now that Acre has elected this ultra-right-wing government."

Alba took us off to her office to meet the gang. It was a small cluttered space, with never quite enough chairs to go round. Our first contact was with Graça, who clearly had better things to do than talk to passing writers. She maintained a harassed expression throughout the interview.

"I'm in charge of the Wildlife Management Program here. We are working with the *seringueiros* at present. Hunting is an important part of their lives, particularly in difficult times like these. It's prohibited, of course, but it's not realistic to expect them to stop. What we want to do is make sure they do it a bit more sensibly. They always go for the same kinds of animal; they hunt right through the breeding season, and they don't have any idea of trying to preserve the females. Then they complain that there isn't the game there used to be! So we go around talking to the families. We're making a calendar and explaining about breeding seasons. We're trying to get them to agree not to hunt in restricted areas, to give the game population a chance to build up. And we are taking a census of the animals they hunt. We give the *seringueiro*'s wife a paper with pictures of the animals: paca, capybara, monkey, armadillo, birds. Every time her husband brings one in, she crosses off the picture of that animal, so we are building up an idea of what there is in there and how many animals they are taking out."

Graça swiftly passed us on to her colleague, Magaly, who had managed to take possession of a chair and was listening in on our conversation.

"I'm working on the hunting survey too," she said. "We do lots of different things in this place. We've just published a map showing the areas in the state that are protected. Take a look at it. It marks the indigenous areas, the national parks, the national forest, the state forest, and the extractive reserves. Of course they're not all going strong, not by any means. The indigenous areas, for instance: There are twenty-five of them marked, but only eleven of those are demarcated, and five of *those* are under dispute for some reason or other—squatters, or the road going through, or settlers arguing about the land, or ranchers claiming some of it. Twelve more are identified, but that doesn't mean that those lands are protected. And two more have yet to be sorted out. Still, it's better than it used to be, and many of those tribes are doing their own demarcation. They're not going to sit around and wait for the government to do it.

"There's a state forest here. It hasn't been legalized yet, but it's going to be funded by the International Tropical Timber Organization for research into forest products. There's one national forest already in place. Not that that means much, but those areas are protected simply because there aren't any roads inside, thank goodness. There's a biological research center down on the border here, and of course the extractive reserves. There are two identified but not expropriated yet, one that hasn't been legalized, and six that have been demarcated and are already operating.

"We've done an atlas of the soil types in the state too. It's important to get the zoning sorted out before they put the road in. We don't want another Rondônia in Acre!

"Of course the new government isn't at all in favor of us in this office. I wouldn't be surprised if we all lose our jobs. I'll tell you why. There was this rancher down near Xapuri who wanted a permit to deforest. When we found out about it, we called a public assembly to protest. Lots of people came; it was the first time anyone had ever called one. The project was reviewed and turned down. We got the reputation of being lefties after that, and that could be a problem with the new government. I think we've lost a good ten years with the election of this governor.

"One of the problems up here is the infighting between national and state organizations. But I must say, they do pull together in times of crisis. I was telling you about the hunting calendar we were making with the *seringueiros,* wasn't I? Well, we're trying to get education and health projects going with them too. We're doing a survey on all aspects of their lives. What they eat, for instance: monkey, tapir, toucan, paca. What they grow: not much, mostly a few onions and manioc. The women take care of the house, the food, the kids. They use some stuff from the forest, but not a lot. The Indians know much more about plants than the *seringueiros* do. Did you know that they still don't use cash? Everything is traded. Everything! And some of the *seringueiros* over in the Juruá couldn't even trade their rubber this year. The price was so low that it wasn't worth anybody's while to go in there and collect it.

"It's funny; the *seringueiros* still seem to have the mentality of slaves. That really gets to me sometimes. But I suppose you can understand it. They lead such isolated lives. They're very conservative—don't like change. Of course, in practical terms, the huge distances also mean that if they get ill—if the cholera came, for instance—they're really too far away to get any help. They'd be dead by the time they got anywhere.

"One of the things that really bugs me is the waste of money around here—all that international aid. They're starting a big new project now. The government of Canada is putting up millions of dollars for the *seringueiros*. It's a nice idea, but the *seringueiros* themselves aren't too happy with it. Nobody ever thought of asking them what they wanted. These people just arrive here with their projects all ready-made and say, 'Well, here they are,' as if they were coming down from heaven or somewhere! I mean, how do they know what's going to work or what isn't? This Canadian project has a special component in it for women. We asked why, and the Canadians said, 'It's because we're putting that into all our projects.' Well we don't want to be just one of their projects. Acre isn't the same as everywhere else. We happen to feel that the people who need a special component in the project aren't the women at all—it's the children.

"The extractive reserves? There's a lot of controversy about them, about whether or not they should make them. Well, I think it's stupid to waste time arguing about that. They're already in place. Of *course* we should have them. What we need to figure out is how the *seringueiros* could get a better deal out of them; what other types of things they could be extracting, and how we could be developing markets for them—that sort of thing.

"You'd better have a word with the boss now. He's the one that keeps us all in line." She introduced us to Jurandir. In his late thirties, he was small and neat. His desk was immaculate, with every last paper clip in place.

"Well, for my sins, I'm the head of this bunch of researchers," he said with a big smile. "But they're not such a bad lot really. I'm the organizer around here. Let me show you the list of our projects.

"It starts with the greening of urban areas. Did you notice that all the trees planted in Rio Branco have signs saying, 'Grow little tree, Acre is waiting for you'? We're also opening ecological centers and making wildlife sanctuaries. There's one up here, have a look on the map. Here. There's a special kind of bee that lives only in this one place in the whole world. It's a bit of a specialty of mine. I'm doing a thesis on it, actually. And there's a project for preserving a particular species of palm; it grows only in one very small area, as far as we know. And then we're making analyses of management plans."

He rummaged around and produced a list of wonderful projects. There were thirteen of them, each carefully listed with the names of the participants, the budget, the physical area of the project, the expected results, the time scheme, and the current status. None of the projects had gotten past the planning stage, but Jurandir wasn't fazed. "We're a little behind," he said, quite unworried. "But we'll get there. You'll see."

Here was another example of the glorious Brazilian optimism that marks roads and hydro schemes on maps years before they are ever constructed. They may *never* be built, but once they're on the map, they exist as far as the Brazilians are concerned. For Jurandir, the existence of this list of projects meant that they were as good as in place already. His bees were safe, his special palm trees would flourish, Rio Branco would be a green and pleasant place, and all his management plans would prosper.

11

A CHORUS OF COMMENTS

Think on these things.
> —St. Paul, Philippians

It's Saturday evening, market day, in Pimenta Buena, Rondônia. The street is flanked by low wooden buildings with peeling paint, sawmills, warehouses, shops, and bars—all unbeautiful but somehow quite purposeful. The market straggles along several blocks. It is the event of the week, and people have come from miles around. People are selling homemade bread, eggs, milk, several different types of cheese, butter, meat, sausage, hams, all sorts of fresh vegetables—manioc, sweet potatoes, yams, potatoes, carrots, cabbage, tomatoes, peppers, eggplants, and lots of unfamiliar tasty-looking leafy green things—bananas, papaya, mangoes, *cupuaçu, guaraná* powder, little bottles of hot chilies, barbecued chicken, tapioca pancakes, manioc cake, coconut candy, bowls of soup, and platefuls of rice and beans. Everything is clean and appetizing.

In one corner is the livestock section: chickens, goats, pigs, and a calf or two. The hardware department has bits for gas rings, handles for saucepans, pocket knives, machetes, scythes, axes, and all manner of nuts, bolts, screws, and nails. Next to it a stall sells twists of sticky black tobacco, horseshoes, hair ribbons, exercise books and pens, plastic buckets and bowls, and a few packets of aspirin. Beyond that is the homemade drink stall with little bottles full of fruit syrups and liqueurs. Next comes the fish stall, the chicken man, the guava paste lady, more sticky cakes, baby clothes, lettuce, milk, medicinal plants and herbs, avocados, bits of material, the saddler, and the man who sells old sacks, ropes, and chains.

Milling happily about are children of all shapes and sizes: blond and blue-eyed descendants of the German settlers in the south, *caboclo* children with straight dark hair and elfin faces, children whose faces are pure Indian or pure African, and any number of variations and combinations of the above. Nobody stares at you as you pass through; this is an immigrant state. Lots of settlers mix in the crowd with Indians, *caboclos*, cattlemen, and loggers. They are all dressed in their best, all set for Saturday night at the bar and perhaps a few games of pool. Parked at one corner of the market are a fleet of ancient buses and a line of pickup trucks—one or two shiny and new, the rest battered and elderly—plus an assortment of horses, mules, motorbikes, bicycles, and hand carts.

Stop at the cheese stall and the people there will tell you how much they like Rondônia. A cheerful lady with her head tied in a blue scarf says, "Oh yes, we do miss the mountains of Paraná. And sometimes I'd like to be really cold for a change. But it's a good life here in Rondônia, and I wouldn't go back now." She sells creamy cheese sauce, fudge, smoked cheese, and fresh cream, if you ask her the week before. The bread lady next door is from Santa Caterina. "No, I haven't got any dark bread. I'm afraid it's all gone. But I'll have some more next Saturday."

Maria dos indios, health project, Rondônia: "I love it here. I wouldn't be anywhere else. Do you know what I like about it? It's the feeling that you can do what you want, say what you think. I love the mist in the mornings rising from the forest. I love the heat. Whenever I go to São Paulo, I can't wait to get home."

Machado, a farmer: "I'm from Minas, but I wouldn't go back there. I love Rondônia. I've built up a *fazenda* here, and I've planted cocoa and coffee. Mind you, if I had to do it now, I'd stick to cattle. Cocoa and coffee, they're too much hard work. Not enough return. Minas? I wouldn't go back to Minas. The people are a tightfisted bunch. I can say that, I'm *mineiro* myself. No, I'd rather be here."

Élio, the ticket clerk at the bus station: "I don't like it. It's too wild up here on the frontier. Everyone's out for something. I'd rather be in the northeast."

Nick, the forester: "I consider myself a Rondônian. I've been here longer than anywhere else. I've made money here and I've lost it. They've tried to kill me. But this is my place. Reckon I'll stick around."

A bar in Porto Velho, state of Rondônia

In the evening light, things look rather melancholy. Perhaps the persistent rain has something to do with it. The bar is on a slight hill, overlooking the river and the railroad terminal where several rusting locomotives lie, their tenders full of logs, waiting for the next dry season when they will transport Sunday visitors. That's not what they were built for; they have more heroic memories than that.

The sun sets over the river. A couple of boats go chugging past. The guitar player plucks a chord or two, then launches into a haunting ballad about the two great Indian nations: Tupi and Guarani. Where are they now?

Charlie, the green-eyed gypsy: "I am Charlie. You like my carvings?" He digs into an ancient shoulder bag and produces a rough but attractive face of the suffering Christ. "Or you prefer something like this?" He rummages again and comes up with a crude figure of a naked lady. "Or this one?" This time he produces a carving of a dolphin. "You know the *boto, si*? You know he come from the river and he steal the young *muchacha*? Well, I was stolen away when I was very *chico*. Charlie was stolen by the gypsies when he was very little—so." He measures with his hands. "I live with the gypsies in the *sertão* for a time, then I run away. I go to Pantanal. You know Pantanal? I live there on a cattle place. I work with cattle. I sleep in hammock and I play my flute to the cattle. They love my music. Everybody love my music. Then one day I come to Rondônia. I travel on the rivers. I have once a canoe. I, Charlie, am sitting in my canoe like this." He demonstrates with the languid grace of a cat. "Playing my flute. And do you know *lo que ocorrio*? The *boto* came and took my flute. Me *roubo*! I say he take it because he like my music. But the music not in the flute. The music in Charlie. So now I don't got my flute no more. But the *boto*, he don't got Charlie's music, either."

Liliane, artist, poet, musician: "There aren't so many of us real Rondônians about. I mean, born in Rondônia, before all these settlers came in. I remember when the road wasn't even tarmacked. It was easier to travel to Manaus by boat than to take the road south, so terrible it used to be. And there wasn't much point. There was nowhere to go to. Well, Porto Velho used to be a quiet little place in those days. There was more going on in Humaitá. Then they put in the roads. It was exciting in a way. Particularly when all those people starting streaming up from the south. You felt you were part of history.

"And then we started to hear about the troubles: fights between the Indians and the settlers, fights between the ranchers and the settlers, fights between the ranchers and the Indians. And they started burning the forest. Before that you didn't really think about the forest. It was there, that was all. And then suddenly they began to cut it. At first it seemed rather exciting, because you were right there when they were actually making history. But then the burning got worse every year. I remember in 1987 the burning season was so bad that there was a haze in the sky for months on end. You could hardly see across the river. There was just a dull brown haze. They used to have to close the airport because the visibility was so poor. And sometimes it made you cough.

"So we decided we must do something about it. We got up protests and marched through the street. We got 3,000 signatures on a petition and gave it to the governor; we had a special Mass in the cathedral; we wrote articles in the paper; we did street theater—everything we could think of. Well, the state government wasn't too worried. After all, it was in favor of developing the state, even if that meant that the forest was knocked down. But slowly people began to be aware of what was happening. The Indians were dying. The settlers couldn't do anything with their plots, half of them. The forest was going up in smoke. And we were all suffocating.

"And then they started the *garimpo* here in the river. Not that there's anything wrong with the *garimpo*. After all, they've been panning gold in these rivers for years. But they started using this mercury. They don't have any idea what they're doing. And nobody does anything about it. Oh yes, the navy told them that they couldn't use the *dragas* right near the town, and they even tried to move them on. But it's not so easy. The *garimpeiros* sneak back at night. You'll even see them sometimes. They drift down here in the dark of the moon, and they'll be gone by morning. It's a tragedy what they've done to this place. And we're all responsible; that's what hurts! We should have realized long ago what was going on. We let ourselves be taken in by the government's big talk about the new frontier. It's a tragedy."

Ana Maria, anthropologist: "You know something? We've had just about enough of people coming up here telling us how to run our business. If it's not people from Brasília, it's people like you! Everybody keeps on at us about the burning of the forest, as though it will be all our fault if the planet gets so hot we all burn up.

"It's all very well for the Americans to blame us like that. What did they do to their forest, I'd like to know? And *their* Indians? And who is responsible for burning all the fossil fuels anyway?

"Yes, what happened in Rondônia *was* a mistake. No question about it. But it couldn't have been foreseen. No one could have stopped those settlers pouring in like that. No one could have known about the soils, that they were so bad. And the business with the Indians. We didn't even know that half of them were there.

"Still, we are trying to clear things up a bit. The burning is much less than it used to be. They've really tightened up on that. And now that they're going to start doing some proper zoning perhaps we'll be able to make something of this place after all."

Veronese, Office of the State Governor: "Poor old Rondônia! We're getting a lot of bad publicity these days. If it's not about the forest it's about the cocaine. Anybody'd think we were living in the Wild West.

"You've got to remember one thing. We're building a state over here—from scratch. And that doesn't happen overnight. We've got to be allowed to settle down.

"We made plenty of mistakes, sure we did. But over a million people are living here now, most of them doing a good sight better than they'd have been doing back home.

"We've got a lot going for us in Rondônia: a huge amount of forest cover, for a start. People will keep telling you how much we've lost, but I bet you don't know how much we still have. Over eighty percent of the state is forest. It's true that they've taken out most of the mahogany and the really good stuff. But we've still got some pretty good stands of pristine forest, and lots of scope for growing forest crops.

"Agriculture, now, that's another thing. We've got a wonderful climate: sunshine all year-round, plenty of rain. It's a dream, really. All we've got to do is figure out what will grow here. We've even got areas of savanna down in the south just made for cattle ranching.

"And we're rich. Look at the cassiterite—largest reserve in the world. There's gold in the rivers, and lots of water in the rivers too. Just think what we can do with all that hydropower.

"I'll tell you something. We're backing the road. No, not the Acre road. The road to the Pacific. Do you know where it's going to go? Through Guajará Mirim into Bolivia, up to La Paz and over to Chile. It'll annoy the hell out of the Acreans, but it's the logical route for it. And you've heard about the new railroad? When that gets built, we're going to be right smack on the export corridor to the Pacific. *Everything* will have to come to Rondônia. It'll take the pressure off the BR-364. We can export all the grains from the center west, all the beef, all our timber and our minerals. When we finish building the new port, this will be the center of the world. Porto Velho is going to be where it's at—on the direct line from São Paulo to Japan."

Rio Branco, the "Casarão," in the state of Acre

Rio Branco is the sort of place you can easily get around on foot—to the interesting parts, anyway. It doesn't have the feel of a river town like Porto Velho, perhaps because the river is rather small and doesn't take much traffic these days. There used to be much more, but they say that the river has silted up a lot since they cut so much forest around the town.

The "Casarão"—Best Beer in Town—is on top of the hill, in the nicer part of town. The main square is up there, with a large military police barracks on one side and opposite it the "Casa do Seringueiro"—a small house painted with murals of the rubber tapper's life. Inside they've got a little museum with a replica of a *caboclo*'s house, and there's a corner where they show videos about the burning of the forest and about the *seringueiros'* struggle. It was here that we talked to Amina about the history of the rubber trade. The place is always crowded in the evenings. Lots of people go there: people who used to be rubber tappers, schoolchildren, people passing by, even the street kids.

Not far from the Casa do Seringueiro is the cathedral. That's where the pastoral lands and the human rights people have their offices. A bit further down the hill is a large ice-cream-cake building that is the State Palace of Government. Built in high classic style in 1930, it sits rather oddly next to the State Bank, an ugly building in neo-concrete-fortress style, circa 1980.

Beyond the square stands a row of two-story office buildings. The ranchers have their offices here; a long line of hopefuls waits outside to see if there are any jobs available. There are several hotels, all rather expensive. Things *are* expensive in Rio Branco. Everything has to come so far to get here, and they don't grow that much in the state. One of the hotels looks like a nineteenth-century saloon out of a Western movie. It's a double-story wooden building on a little dirt side street. The inside is spotlessly clean, with lace doilies everywhere and little tinsel hangings that must have been left over from Christmas. Every available surface has a vase of plastic flowers on it; the hotel owner gets up early each morning to put one fresh hibiscus in each vase. Each evening he wheels out two television sets. The upstairs one is switched to the local channel; the downstairs one shows the national news. The residents sit on the front veranda, fanning themselves and watching life straggle past.

But the Casarão is where people meet in the evening. It's a cozy, inward-looking place—the sort of place where you automatically scan the tables to see who is there. You don't look out to the street because there isn't much to see out there, except the military barracks directly in front. The Casarão is next to the telephone office, where everybody turns up sooner or later. The beer is cheap, and it serves the best pizza in town. It's a great place for hanging out.

Rubens Branquinho, businessman (narrowly lost the race for state governor): "I'm a peaceful soul. What all these ecologists and inter- fering busybodies want to do is to finish off this state. We're fight- ing to make it a better place, to put a stop to misery and isolation, to get electricity and roads. And they do nothing but insult us!"

Paulo Enrique, lawyer, landowner: "The road is all ready for tar- macking, you know. It's going to revolutionize the state. Just think, we'll be able to send out our wood, our beef. This is going to be the richest state in the whole of Brazil."

Ricardo, the Lutheran pastor: "I'm actually hoping to get into the school of anthropology. Do you know what I want to study? I want to look at all these medicinal plants: *ayahuasca,* for one. You know, the stuff they use in the Santo Daime rituals. Yes, I have tried it once—very pleasant, not at all threatening. Of course this place is riddled with drugs, rotten with them. They're growing *epadu,* that's shade-grown cocaine, in the Juruá valley. It's much more profitable than tapping rubber. And they have those *mescla* cigarettes here. Have you tried them? You don't smoke? Well, that's probably wise. They're made from marijuana and coca paste, and they come from Guajará Mirim.

"There's a terrific trade between the Mafia and the Peruvian Sendero Luminoso guerillas in the Cruzeiro area. The Mafia pro- vides food and arms in exchange for drugs. There are lots of dif- ferent ways for the drugs to come in. The borders are pretty porous. So are the customs, if it comes to that! They bring the stuff by river to Cruzeiro, or by air. They bring it through Guajará Mirim, along the Abuna River, up to Rio Branco, and then to Brasília by air. There are factories in Guajará Mirim where they process the stuff. Then it goes down the BR-364. That's why they call it the TransCoca Highway. It's not difficult to get rich around here if you're in the right business."

Reynaldo, lives on an extractive reserve, formerly worked with the British charitable organization Oxfam UK): "Yes, well, I've got my own holding in the middle of the Chico Mendes Reserve. Yes, of course the *seringueiros* think I'm crazy. I'm trying to run a one-man demonstration plot, if you like. What I want to do is reduce their dependence on the traders by doing more subsistence planting. There are lots of things they could be growing, but usually they don't bother with much. They waste a lot of land too. They clear it for pasture, and then the *capoeira* comes in, and the cattle won't touch it, so they have to clear a bit more. They burn the *capoeira*, but it's fierce stuff, and it always comes back. I'm trying to show them how they could cut it and use it as fertilizer instead of burning it. And I'm experimenting with raising cattle semiconfined. I'm planting trees in mixed stands and doing a bit of reforestry. I'm trying out all sorts of vegetables and a bit of rice too. It's a lot of work, but they're getting used to me now, and one day they'll come to see that there is something in what I'm trying to do. But things move very slowly. They're not used to change, you see. Basically, very little has changed for them, and they tend to think that changes are usually for the worse!"

Xapuri, Acre

The streets of Xapuri are full of people looking at you curiously. No one smiles. There's nothing to buy. A row of wooden shacks is perched along the waterfront. At the end is a handsome wooden building that used to be the Bolivian Customs post at the time of Acre's glorious revolution. The little place that offers "lanches" doesn't serve anything until evening. A sloppy youth digs into a cold chest and produces a glass of *cupuaçu* juice. It has a delicious Amazônian flavor, unlike anything else. One could do with at least three times the amount. "Filtered?" he asks in disbelief. "The water? Filtered? No it isn't. These days we aren't even getting water out of the tap." A glance at the muddy river behind is enough to fill the stoutest heart with dismay. There's a cholera epidemic just across the border in Peru. The first cases are expected here any day.

The office of the rubber tappers' union is a small shabby room with a shelf of dusty books, an electric typewriter with its cord hitched over a beam, a large portrait of Chico Mendes, a TV, a silver clock, and a fan. A cavernous back room contains several hammocks, a gas stove with big shiny cooking pots on it, and an old freezer full of bottles of water.

Osmar, the union leader, walks us through the breathless heat of the afternoon to the Brazil nut factory. It's a shiny new building. Inside, rows of women and children are operating the nut-cracking presses. "It's better done by women. They don't break so many," the manager says. The nuts are sun-dried, kiln-dried, tested for the correct humidity content, opened—laboriously—and packed into foil-lined boxes for export to the United States. The funding comes from an American company.

The cooperative is in a large dark warehouse on the waterfront. A few *seringueiros* sit, hats in laps, waiting to talk to the bored-looking young man who is listlessly writing details of something into a notebook. A few flies, drugged by the stupefying heat, flap about. We are all mopping our brows. The slightest exertion, like getting up out of your chair, causes the sweat to run down inside your shirt and down your legs.

The hotel is one of those dispiriting establishments where everything smells of urine, and little piles of dirt lurk in all the corners. The owner, an untidy woman, indicates a room with a dusty air conditioner at a price one might expect to pay for something considerably cleaner in Rio Branco. The eating arrangements look depressingly unhygienic, and the little yard behind the kitchen is full of vultures.

Six o'clock is happy hour. If you sit on the wooden bench outside the hotel's front door, it is marginally cooler than inside. Warm soda can be had, at exorbitant expense. Several people appear to be living in the hotel permanently. One is a young obstetrician from Peru. She is working in the town hospital and visiting the health posts. She wants to get to know Brazil. I hope she doesn't think it's all like this! Another resident is a middle-aged veterinarian from Ceará. Everyone seems to be from Ceará. Can anybody still be living there? He is working in public health. Public health? Does he know there's no water coming out of the taps? Although, to be fair, there *is* something coming out of the tap in the hotel room, but not anything you would want to take a shower in. The vet says he finds Xapuri a bit rough. One of his jobs is to inspect the meat supply. "Last week I found them slaughtering an ox on the bank of the river, right in the town," he told me wearily. "I said to them, 'You can't do that, you're supposed to slaughter in the slaughterhouse,' and they just waved their knives at me and told me to shove off."

Cesar, veterinary technician: "Yes, well, I'm from Xapuri. I started the very first feed and veterinary medicine shop three years back. There wasn't anything before. But there isn't much business. Nobody's got any money, you see, except the ranchers. And they mostly get their stuff from Rio Branco. Do you know what I'd really like to do? I'm going to run for mayor in the next elections. There's so much that needs to be done here. You can see for yourself. No sanitation, terrible roads, precarious health service. The schools are dreadful. The whole place is a ruin. My father says that when he was young things were much better. And have you seen the way everybody keeps looking over their shoulders all the time? You never feel really safe here, that's what it is. You never know who's listening, where the next bullet is going to come from. We've got to get this place cleaned up. We can't have these *pistoleiros* walking freely about the place like this. It's like the Wild West!

"Another thing. We'll have to do something about the voting system. All the candidates go around buying votes with T-shirts, mattresses, gas cylinders, sometimes even chain saws. And of course everybody knows who everyone's voting for. Something like seventy percent of the voters here work for the administration—federal or state or municipal. There's no secret vote. It takes real courage to vote for the Workers' Party, for instance.

"I don't think I have a hope of winning, but I'm going to give it a try."

Shirlene, Cesar's wife: "You want to know what I think about this place? It stinks, that's what. Nothing ever happens here. There are no facilities. It's always hot as hell and full of *pium* [sand flies]. And I'm allergic to them. My legs are covered with bites. I have to wear jeans all the time, even in this heat. When Chico was alive it was different. It was pretty miserable then too, but at least you felt that things were happening. He wanted me to go and work in the Projeto Seringueiro, but it didn't work out—not for me, I mean. Sometimes I feel that nothing's ever going to happen in this place, except killings. If Cesar doesn't get elected, we're leaving."

We sat on the veranda of Cesar and Shirlene's house in the heavy atmosphere of a Xapuri night. Cesar glanced over his shoulder every few minutes. It made me uneasy, and I found myself peering out into the ill-lit street, wondering who might be lurking there.

In Xapuri the two sides in the Amazon drama were confronting each other head on. I could feel, in my skin, the menace of the situation. Paradoxically, it is in Xapuri and places like it that the forest people are stitching together a new future for themselves.

Chico Mendes had been killed on just such a night, only a few yards from where I was sitting. Others would die. Yet there were enough people concerned about the forest and its people to make sure that it wasn't the end. I found myself believing that things would get better.

I remembered what Chico had written shortly before he died: "My dream is to see this entire forest conserved because we know it can guarantee the future of all the people who live in it. Not only that, I believe that in a few years the Amazon can become an economically viable region, not only for us, but for the whole nation, for all of humanity, and for the whole planet."

Chico is dead. His place has been taken by Osmarino Amancio. Osmarino is under no illusions about the forest:

"We may be illiterates isolated in the middle of the forest," he said, "but we do know what's going on. We know that livestock doesn't work here, and we know which other things will, but we don't have the technical ways of explaining it.

"We need people who can help us evaluate natural resources, how to market products so we can get a better price, ways to get better cooperatives going. We know that rubber and other extractive products can sustain a community without destroying the forest."

And then I thought of what one of the Kayapó chiefs had written: "The forest is one big thing. It has people, animals, and plants.

There is no point saving the forest if the people and animals who live in it are killed or driven away.

"The groups trying to save the race of animals cannot win if the people trying to save the forest lose; the people trying to save the Indians cannot win if either of the others lose; the Indians cannot win without the support of these groups; but the groups cannot win without the help of the Indians, who know the forest and the animals and can tell what is happening to them.

"No one of us is strong enough to win alone; together we can be strong enough to win."

12

WHAT NEXT?

If it were done when 'tis done, then 'twere well it were done quickly.

—William Shakespeare, *Macbeth*

Juliet and I had spent three months with the forest people. We had tramped through the forest with the rubber tappers, chatted with the Indians in their *malocas*, waited in an endless succession of bus stations, and roared over atrocious roads in ancient and decrepit vehicles. We had seen a lot of Rondônia and a lot of Acre, and now that we were back at our *fazenda*, it was time to pull it all together.

I remembered the milkman back in England: "It's a real shame what they're doing to the forest and all those Indians." And I remembered Dona Lara and her family, who had made themselves a new life in Acre. I thought of the dispossessed rubber tappers and of the herds of white cattle that had replaced them. I thought of the giant tree trunks in the lumber yard and of Nick with his mahogany seedlings. I thought of the silence of the rivers where the dolphins played, and of the din and dirt of the dredgers. I thought of the ruined fields under the smoke pall of the burning season, and of the brave new wooden houses with their ragged hopeful families.

Things didn't seem so black and white anymore. The forest people wanted one thing and the outsiders wanted exactly the opposite. Was there any way of bringing change and bettering people's lives without bringing devastation?

I started by thinking about the Indians. They are the biggest losers. They have lost their lands, their livings, and their lives. For them nothing is more urgent than the demarcation and protection of their lands. Only when this has been done will they gain a breathing space to consider which aspects of the white man's world they wish to adopt.

Some of the white man's things will be vital to them. Their health patterns have been drastically altered, so they need access to better health care. Contact with the white world puts them at a disadvantage for lack of formal education, so they need to have schools—although they would like to have some control over what is taught in them, so that they can preserve their language and culture. Since they are now more or less participating in the market economy, they want to be able to market their products fairly and receive decent prices for them. As they come inexorably closer to the white man's world, they must find the self-confidence to value their own culture and traditions. Their knowledge of forest ways is a valuable heritage for us all; it is important that both we and they are aware of this. One hopeful sign is the establishment of an Indigenous Center in the state of Goiás, where the Union of Indigenous Nations is attempting to collect traditional Indian knowledge and pass it on to other Indians.

Antonio Apurinã remarked, "We have to make our place in your world." Like it or not, they must. But as the Indians make this difficult and delicate transition, they need to feel secure about their lands, they need time to come to terms with what he described as "this wrenching change," and they need the information and confidence to make their own decisions. "We want to speak for ourselves," Antonio said.

They may choose to sell their mahogany to the loggers. Should they so choose, they must understand the full implications of that choice. The government needs to exercise strict control over the whole process, making certain that the Indians get a fair deal.

I tried to see the situation through the loggers' eyes. "These forests were given to us by God to be used. I get in there. I get out the good trees. I move on." But Armando from the Seringueiros' Council thought the opposite. "Whatever happens, we've got to make sure that Acre stays under forest."

We can't expect the entire Amazon logging industry to stop cold. Even if that were desirable, it would be unenforceable. What

has to be done is to make sure that sustainable forest industries
become more financially attractive than those that are not. As
more and more of the world's ancient forests are cut, the value of
this last great rain forest will increase. Therefore it is essential that
the Brazilian government recognize the enormous value of the
standing forests and take steps to protect them. Logging in primary areas should be strictly controlled and preferably phased
out altogether. Such strict control would start with careful evalua-
tion of the road-building program, remembering that roads bring
people and people bring deforestation. In areas where controlled
logging is permitted, serious stumpage fees must be levied, accompanied by vigorous programs of enrichment planting.

The current, highly wasteful method of wood processing presents another set of problems. The loggers pointed out the difficul-
ties in getting parts and maintenance for machinery, the unreliable
energy supplies, and the chronic shortage of skilled labor. These
problems can be solved by the loggers themselves if they believe
that it is worth their while. One way to increase the value of their
finished products would be to set up small-scale manufacturing.
The manufacture of good-quality products would generate employment, keep profits within the region, and create a profitable
export market—particularly if their products were certified as
coming from properly managed forests.

Sustainable logging goes hand in hand with reforestry. The
forester in Acre put it simply, "Instead of paying ranchers to clear
huge chunks of forestland, the government should be paying people to keep their land under forest and start replanting on the degraded lands." Ranchers could be weaned away from their unprofitable and destructive cattle raising into planting industrial forests,
sweetened by the financial incentives that were formerly used for
cattle. These plantations could be providing wood for construction,
charcoal, pulp, and fuel. Smaller landowners could be signed up to
participate in mixed agroforestry, in combinations of forestry and
pasture, in rotation of woodland crops, in nurseries for reforestry
and enrichment planting, and in the creation of germ banks for
pupunha, cupuaçu, jaborandi, Brazil nuts, cocoa, guaraná, araçá,
babaçu, dendé, acaí, and other species. Agroforestry projects could
benefit the river populations, *seringueiros,* big and small landowners, and research and extension people. There is no shortage of

suitable land; Amazônia possesses around twelve million acres of degraded lands. Best of all, ample money is available from bilateral and multilateral aid programs to fund this sort of program.

Climate change was one of the world's chief concerns at the Earth Summit in Rio. The richer countries committed millions of dollars to financing forestry schemes. This was not simply because they like the idea of miles and miles of forest. To Northern countries the reforesting of the Amazon makes economic sense. It also delays painful political decisions about reducing carbon emissions at home. If for no other reason, it would pay to reforest the Amazon purely in terms of its function as a carbon sink. In December 1991, *The Economist* published the following information on the cost of various means of preventing one ton of CO_2 from entering the atmosphere:

- Control deforestation in the Amazon—$4
- Cut U.S. emissions by 10 percent (cars, factories)—$10
- Reforest Amazônia—$30
- Cut U.S. emissions by 50 percent—$130

As for the areas of permanent preservation, what better way to maintain their integrity than by making the forest people themselves act as their guardians, taking advantage of their knowledge of species and ecosystems and permitting them to make sustainable use of the areas by extracting forest products? "We may be illiterates isolated in the middle of the forest, but we do know what's going on," said Osmarino, the rubber tappers' leader from Xapuri. "We know that livestock doesn't work here, and we know which other things will."

My thoughts turned to the river people. Their basic desires are simple. They want to be able to achieve a reasonable standard of living so that they will no longer be obliged to go off to the cities or the *garimpos*. Dona Morena and Pedro had talked about what their community lacked. Dona Morena was concerned about health care, particularly the inadequate supply of medicines and transport facilities in cases of medical emergencies. One reason for the river people's generally low level of health is their lack of access to clean water and sanitation. These could be remedied at the village level by building septic tanks and providing water filters.

Pedro had also put his finger on one of the more subtle problems facing them: "There are a lot of changes in the river itself too, partly because of the forest being cut. The whole pattern of flooding is changing, and since we grow most of our food on the floodplains, that's serious." Although it will be hard for the river people to change the flood patterns of the river, they could increase their food production on the floodplains with more help from the agricultural extension technicians. They could also be encouraged to try fish farming. Fish are highly nutritious and provide valuable skins for making leather. Raising ornamental fish could be good business, and farming other animals such as turtles, alligators, capybaras, and pacas could provide another source of profit and protein.

I thought of the terrible contradictions of Amazônia, of the miserable poverty and the staggering riches, both biological and mineral. And I remembered the terrible damage done by the gold miners, both to themselves and to the environment. Ludwig had put it succinctly. "As for the *garimpeiros,* all they are doing is throwing away their money, ruining their health, and poisoning the rivers."

What is the solution? Perhaps the government's idea of creating *garimpo* reserves would be worth trying. The *garimpeiros* would have better operating conditions, and the traditional people would be protected from *garimpeiro* encroachments. Under the controlled conditions of a reserve, *garimpeiros* could have access to cooperatives, health services, technical assistance, and improved security. Restricted access would help prevent many of the social evils that currently surround the *garimpo.* The government would also be able to capture significantly better revenues through taxing the sale of gold.

Unemployed *garimpeiros* could be absorbed by the mining companies, where conditions would be better and safer, and more money would find its way into the state coffers. It would also be considerably easier for the authorities to insist on environmental rehabilitation of mined areas.

What about the settlers? Veronese had stated, "We want our farmers to make a better living." The quickest way to achieve that would be to increase production. Farmers need help in assessing the best possible uses for their land, and they need inputs including credit, marketing, fair pricing, and improved transport to realize its full potential. Existing roads will need to be properly maintained and the construction of new ones restricted to discourage spontaneous migration. Settlers should be encouraged to grow food for local use and to try agroforestry, fish raising, and small-scale livestock production. "It's not as though we need more agricultural land," said Nick. "What we need is better technology."

I thought about the ranchers. "Brazil needs people like us," one of them had told me. Indeed Brazil does. The ranchers supply a fund of cash, intelligence, and drive that needs to be used more productively. After all, they are basically entrepreneurs. Cattle raising could be restricted to small semi-intensive areas and the cattle fed on agricultural wastes, which is something that Reynaldo is trying on the *seringal* in Acre.

Since extensive cattle raising is the worst possible alternative in Amazônia, the government should not permit any new cattle projects to be set up and should maintain strict controls over deforestation on private property. The energy and enthusiasm of the entrepreneurs could more profitably be channeled into large-scale forestry projects, together with the manufacture and export of forest products. Rubens Branquinho had put it this way: "We're fighting to make Acre a better place, to put a stop to misery and isolation, and to get electricity and roads." Forestry projects could provide the employment and the cash to achieve this.

What about the rubber tappers? They need land security, health care, fair prices for their products, and help with diversification—the extraction of other products such as medicinal plants, fruits, resins, oils, and essences. They will flourish best on the extractive reserves, particularly because they will then be able to set up cooperatives for marketing their products. "If we didn't have a boss we wouldn't have to pay rent," Chico had told us, "and we'd be able to sell our rubber through a cooperative like they do in Xapuri. They get better prices than we do and they buy their supplies more cheaply."

The rubber tappers could also become involved in processing as they are in Boca do Acre, where they now produce artificial leather (made from latex-covered sugar sacks). The material is then sent to Rio to be made up into high-quality bags, briefcases, and the like. Maybe they could get involved in processing other forest products—candies and preserves from forest fruits, gums and essences, and handicrafts.

The *seringueiros* are also interested in enriching their forests. "People are starting to think about how we could be using other forest products as well," said Osmar, the union leader. "We could be planting things like *guaraná* and cocoa, and even putting in new rubber trees." Enriching their forests could include better care of the wildlife. The *seringueiros*, too, could set up small-scale projects raising capybara, paca, alligators, and fish.

In order to bring about these changes, institutions will have to be strengthened. The derelict Indian agency FUNAI should be better financed. Forest people must be encouraged to participate in community affairs, and infrastructure everywhere has to be upgraded. "There's so much that needs to be done here," said Cesar from Xapuri, "You can see for yourself. No sanitation, terrible roads, precarious health service. The schools are dreadful. The whole place is a ruin."

Flagging local economies could receive the kiss of life through small industries based on local resources: bioindustry, agroindustry, pharmaceuticals, cosmetics, food. Reforestry on a large scale will create thousands of jobs, and international money will be available for funding through debt-for-nature swaps, bilateral or multilateral aid, and grants. The South is still dependent on the North for technology, cash, and markets, but there are signs that the South is asserting itself, particularly in the wake of the Earth Summit.

One of the subjects addressed at the summit was technology transfer. Money will be available for the transfer of environmentally benign technologies, and it is essential that these transfers be accompanied by an adequate training and follow-up program.

The question of preserving biodiversity remains crucial. It is also Amazônia's trump card. With properly administered forest reserves guarded by traditional forest people, and with bioindustries, biotechnological industries, and research centers in the region, Amazônia will be able to realize its true vocation as a treasure house of bioriches. Fortunately for Amazônia, it is not too late.

What is the role of the Brazilian government in all this? It must implement land zoning and eliminate financial incentives for ranching, transferring them to forestry. It must invest in wood processing and industrialization. The government must improve infrastructure in all areas and encourage clean, up-to-date, and appropriate technology. It has to be firm on the issue of the *garimpo*. Finally, it must invest in education at all levels, particularly environmental education, and provide assistance to migrants so they can integrate into Amazônian life.

Moreover, training and decent salaries should be made available to competent development professionals, and special emphasis should be placed on the dissemination of ecologically sound practices. Scientific knowledge available outside the region could be imported to regional research centers, and contacts and cooperation with other Amazônian countries should be encouraged. Foreign money should continue to be used in research, forest inventories, satellite monitoring, and new uses for forest products—with particular emphasis on bioindustries such as those being studied at FUNTAC in Acre.

Perhaps most importantly, since the future of Amazônia depends on its people, they must be involved. They should be included in decisionmaking; lured into small, sustainable projects; and established in small industries. Control and responsibility for the land belong in the hands of its people.

What about the internationals? They should be giving serious attention to the question of debt relief. It's unrealistic to expect hard-pressed Southern countries to pay proper attention to environmental preservation when they are desperately trying to come up with the dollars to pay off the interest on their never-ending debt. Southern countries need a better deal in terms of international trade, which is traditionally weighted against them, and they need fair access to protected Northern markets. They need clean technology that is made available to them on reasonable terms. They would like more control over the international funding agencies, which they believe are manipulated by the North to influence Southern policy decisions. And Southern NGOs need all the support they can get from their Northern colleagues in pressuring their governments to ensure that human and environmental rights are adequately monitored and respected.

My thoughts came back to the milkman, so far away. What could I tell him, if he wanted to know how to stop them cutting down the forest? I could tell him to use his consumer power. I could tell him to ascertain that the forest products that he might buy—such as a piece of wooden furniture or a jar of face cream for his wife—were made from certified forest products. I could tell him about the campaign that Friends of the Earth mounted to boycott nonsustainably produced timber. I could tell him that things will get better as long as people like him keep up the pressure and support any organization that can prove that it is working effectively to improve the lot of the forest people.

EPILOGUE

The United Nations Conference on Environment and Development (UNCED), better known as the Earth Summit, was held in Rio de Janeiro in June 1992. It set itself a formidable mandate, nothing less than how to save our earth from destruction. "Only one world," it proclaimed in myriad languages. "Care and share. The future is in our hands."

With this in mind, 15,000 official government delegates came to the Earth Summit to debate the question of how we can all share the earth without destroying it. The press corps was 9,000 strong—the largest press corps ever assembled. The parallel people's environmental conference, the '92 Global Forum, was attended by over half a million people.

Tommy Koh, chairperson of the Earth Summit Preparatory Committee, spoke for them all. "The people of the world have two wishes on environment and development," he said. "We wish to live happy and meaningful lives in dignity and sufficiency. We also wish to live in harmony with nature. The challenge for Rio is to reconcile these two wishes for the sake of our children and their children. We must not fail."

Present in Rio were heads of state; delegates from governments, UN agencies, and multilateral development agencies; representatives from business associations, trade unions, scientific and academic bodies, religious groups, associations of indigenous people, women, young people, and non-government organizations (NGOs) from around the world. While the official government conference was in progress, the '92 Global Forum—the People's Summit—was taking place across town. It was, in its own words, "a unique, unprecedented gathering of world citizens concerned about the fate of their planet and determined to make their opinions known when and where it counts." Never before have so many people come together to discuss the fate of the earth.

In preparation for UNCED, public forums were held in Mexico City, Buenos Aires, Moscow, Amsterdam, Nairobi, New Delhi, and Cairo. Each participating country was asked to submit a national report to serve as a basis for discussion in the four official preparatory meetings that were held over a two-year period prior to the conference. In theory, agreements were to be hammered out during these preconference meetings; in practice, negotiations continued right up to the eve of the signings in Rio.

Subjects discussed at the Earth Summit included poverty; protecting the atmosphere; climate change and energy use; desertification; forests; sustainable agriculture; biodiversity and biotechnology; water supplies; toxic chemicals; hazardous waste; oceans; fresh water; environmental education; technology transfer; the rights and contributions to development of indigenous peoples, women and youth; and institutional, trading, and financing mechanisms to support sustainable development.

Five main documents were adopted by governments at the Earth Summit:

- **The Rio Declaration** stated the basic principles: that people are central to sustainable development; that states hold sovereign rights over their natural resources; and that the rate of development must not exceed the capacity of the earth to renew itself, nor prejudice its future capacity to do so. It also stated that Southern countries should have priority in development, that all countries should cooperate to share knowledge and technology, and that polluters should pay the cost of cleaning up.

- **Agenda 21** provides a blueprint for action in all areas relating to sustainable development from now into the twenty-first century. "Humanity stands at a defining moment in its history. We can continue with present policies that are perpetuating the economic gap within and between countries, increasing poverty, hunger, sickness and illiteracy worldwide, and causing the continued deterioration of the ecosystems on which we depend to sustain life on earth. Or we can change course, bringing improved living standards to all, better protected and managed ecosystems, and a safer, more prosperous future. No nation can achieve this on its own. Together we can, in a global partnership for sustainable development."

- **The Climate Convention** came to general agreements on reducing carbon emissions, but stopped short of setting levels and timetables.

- **The Biodiversity Convention** (christened by one weary delegate the Mother of All Conventions) discussed ways to preserve the richness of life, its ecosystems, species, and genetic diversities. It also took up the thorny issues of biotechnology, intellectual property rights, patenting of life forms, and possible consequences of genetic engineering.

- **The Statement of Forest Principles** asserts that nations have sovereign rights to exploit their forests, but that they should use proper management techniques. Large sums of money will be made available for conservation and reforestry.

Agreements were reached on the transfer of technology and funds and the establishment of a UN Commission on Sustainable Development.

Noel Brown, U.S. head of United Nations Environmental Program, described himself as "a radical optimist, because I believe that humanity is an extremely creative problem-solving species and we are a generation that is capable of conceiving the earth as a whole."

Maurice Strong, Coordinator of UNCED, observed, "Some say that expectations for this conference have been too high. They cannot be too high. Saving the earth and making it a better and more hospitable place for future generations is an achievable goal. The only barrier is us."

Martin Khor spoke for the Third World Network, a highly active Southern NGO dealing with environmental and developmental issues, based in Malaysia. "The South is saying: You want us to cut down on our use of industry because of CO_2 emission. You don't want us to cut down trees, you want us to have sustainable development on a per capita income of $500 a year, but you are continuing at $18,000 and you want more. You are taking more and more of the world's resources and asking us to pay for it by limiting our use of resources. That is unacceptable. And that is the crux of UNCED."

Warren Lindner, coordinator of the '92 Global Forum, rejoiced that "we have people from all over the world speaking out. It's a voice that never was heard before."

As delegates in Rio were huddling over the final details of Earth Summit negotiations, over at the '92 Global Forum the NGOs were equally busy. They were holding regional workshops, cultural exchanges, and plenary discussions. They were lobbying official delegates and drawing up their own alternative treaties, in which they pledged themselves to certain courses of action and undertook to pressure their governments to do likewise. Again and again people expressed their desire for demilitarization, an end to nuclear testing and the export of hazardous waste, and much firmer restrictions on the use of chemicals in agriculture. People want to support the groups that they perceive as marginalized: indigenous peoples, women, and children. They want fair trade terms for the South, debt relief, and reduced consumption in Northern countries. They don't want the Green Fund to be controlled by the World Bank, which, they point out, has a poor environmental record as well as a culture of arrogance and secrecy. They have a profound respect for cultural, biological, and spiritual diversity, and they are generally opposed to attempts to manipulate nature through patenting of living organisms.

The Rio experience gave voice to the concern by thousands of people for the future of the earth. In the end, the very fact that so many of them came together may turn out to be more important than what was decided. It was a massive gesture of solidarity among the peoples of the planet; a Vietnamese delegate called it a "most eloquent commitment of nations to strive for a new world of peace, justice, equity, solidarity and development in harmony with nature."

This was the first world summit at which the superpowers did not play a major role: the USSR had disintegrated, and the United

States played only a peripheral part—although U.S. citizens were high-profile participants in the '92 Global Forum and lobbied their government vigorously but unsuccessfully throughout.

To Maurice Strong, both the Earth Summit and the '92 Global Forum were "a great success." But for Danny Kennedy of Australia who spoke for Youth Forum, the Earth Summit was "a total failure, because it will not and cannot deal with poverty on one side and overconsumption on the other."

Chief Oren Lyon of the Onandaga Nation described it as "an extraordinary time and an extraordinary meeting."

Prime Minister Felipe Gonzales of Spain pointed out that "five hundred years ago man discovered earth's dimension, and in Rio he has discovered its limits."

One of the most eloquent statements to come out of the summit was the Earth Charter drawn up by the NGOs. They are pressing for the UN to adopt this charter on the occasion of its fiftieth birthday in 1995. The document begins thus:

We are Earth, the people, plants and animals,
rains and oceans,
breath of the forest and flow of the sea.
We honor Earth as the home of all living things.
We cherish Earth's beauty and diversity of life.
We welcome Earth's ability to renew as being the basis of all life.
We recognize the special place of Earth's Indigenous Peoples,
their territories, their customs,
and their unique relationship to Earth.
We are appalled at the human suffering, poverty and
damage to Earth
caused by inequality of power.
We accept a shared responsibility to protect and
restore Earth
and to allow wise and equitable use of resources
so as to achieve an ecological balance
and new social, economic and spiritual values.
In all our diversity we are one.
Our common home is increasingly threatened.

It is in our hands.

BIBLIOGRAPHY

Binswanger, Hans. 1987. *Fiscal and Legal Incentives with Environmental Effects on the Brazilian Amazon.* Washington, D.C.: World Bank.

Binswanger, Hans. 1989. *Brazilian Policies that Encourage Deforestation in the Amazon.* Washington, D.C.: World Bank.

Brown, Lester, Christopher Flavin, and Sandra Postel. 1992. *Saving the Planet.* New York: W. W. Norton.

Burns, E. Bradford. 1980. *A History of Brazil.* New York: Columbia University Press.

Caufield, Catherine. 1985. *In the Rainforest.* New York: Knopf.

Collins, Mark, ed. 1990. *The Last Rainforests.* London: Mitchell Beazley.

Commission on Development and Environment for Amazonia. 1992. *Amazonia without Myths.* Geneva: United Nations Development Program, Inter-American Development Bank, Amazon Cooperation Treaty.

Denslow, Julie Sloan, and Christine Padoch. 1988. *People of the Tropical Rainforest.* Berkeley: University of California Press.

Economist, The. 1991. "A Survey of Brazil: Drunk Not Sick." December 7–13, pp. 1–22.

Gregersen, Hans, Sydney Draper, and Dieter Elz. 1989. *People and Trees.* Washington, D.C.: Economic Development Institute, World Bank.

Grzybowski, Candido. 1989. *O Testamento do Homem da Floresta.* Rio de Janeiro: FASE.

Gunther, John. 1967. *Inside South America.* London: Hamish Hamilton.

Hecht, Susannah, and Alexander Cockburn. 1989. *The Fate of the Forest: Developers, Destroyers and Defenders of the Amazon.* London and New York: Verso.

145

Hemming, John. 1978. *Red Gold*. London: Murray.

Kelly, Brian, and Mark London. 1983. *Amazon*. New York: Harcourt, Brace and Jovanovich.

Kricher, John. 1989. *A Neotropical Companion*. Princeton, N.J.: Princeton University Press.

Le Breton, Juliet. 1991. "Common Sense: The Role of Community Management for Rain Forest Conservation in Latin America." B.Sc. diss., University College, London.

Mahar, Dennis. 1989. *Government Policies and Deforestation in Brazil's Amazon Region*. Washington, D.C.: World Bank.

McNeely, Jeffery A., Kenton R. Miller, Walter V. Reid, Russell A. Mittermeier, and Timothy B. Werner. 1990. *Conserving the World's Biological Diversity*. Gland, Switzerland, and Washington, D.C.: International Union for the Conservation of Nature and Natural Resources, World Resources Institute, Conservation International, World Wildlife Fund–US, and World Bank.

Mee, Margaret. 1988. *In Search of Plants of the Rainforest*. Woodbridge, England: Nonesuch Expeditions.

Mendes, Chico. 1989. *Fight for the Forest: Chico Mendes in His Own Words*. London: Latin America Bureau.

Myers, Norman. 1985. *The Primary Source: Tropical Forests and Our Future*. New York: Norton.

Repetto, Robert. 1988. *Economic Policy Reforms for Natural Resource Conservation*. Washington, D.C.: World Bank.

Revkin, Andrew. 1990. *The Burning Season*. London: Collins.

Rizzini, Carlos Toledo, Adelmar F. Coimbra, and Antonio Houaiss. 1988. *Ecosistemas Brasileiras*. Rio de Janeiro: Editora Index.

Shoumatoff, Alex. 1978. *The Rivers Amazon*. London: Century Books.

Spears, John. 1988. *Containing Tropical Deforestation*. Washington, D.C.: World Bank.

Sterling, Thomas. 1973. *The Amazon*. Amsterdam: Time-Life Books.

Veja. 1989. "Minério na superficie." Edition 1086 (July 5), pp. 86–96.

Wilson, E. O., ed. 1988. *Biodiversity*. Washington, D.C.: National Academy Press.

World Bank. 1992. *World Development Report*. Washington, D.C.: World Bank.

World Commission on Environment and Development. 1987. *Sustainable Development*. Geneva: Centre for Our Common Future.

INDEX

Abacaxi, 47
Acre, 6, 7–8, 12, 32, 66, 77
   Acre Purus, 105
   land titling in, 78, 85
   River Acre, 64
Agroforestry, 27, 74, 132
Alliance of the Forest Peoples, 20
Amancio, Osmarino, 128, 133
Amazônia, 1–4
Ariquemes, 62
Atmospheric CO_2, 133

Belém, 42, 95
Benchimol, Samuel, 73
Biodiversity, 136
Biodiversity Convention, 141
Biological resources, 2–3
Boca do Acre, 135
Bolivia, 54, 56, 97
Bom Futuro, 27
BR-364, 4, 6, 21, 44, 46, 59, 60, 74

Brasília, 1, 12, 14, 19, 57, 100, 106
Brazil
   Brazilian beef, 7–8, 80–81
   concept of Greater, 3, 6, 60
   forestry code, 28–29
   forestry management, 31–33
   gross domestic product (GDP), 80
   land reform issues, 84–86

Cabanagem rebellion, 42
Cabeça Seca, 17
Caboclos, 8, 18, 19–20, 32, 36, 42, 77, 81
Caciques, 16
Cacoal, 61, 63
Caiado, Ronaldo, 85
Calama, 34–44
Canada, 115
Candirus, 91
CAPEMI, 22, 23

Capoeiras, 63, 74, 79
Casarão, 122–25
Cassiterite mining, 6, 36, 44
Cattle, 63, 79, 82–83, 135
 Brazilian beef, 7–8, 80–81
Chicha, 16
Chimarrão, 70
Churches, 44, 65, 69, 97–98
 liberation theology, 104–5
Climate change, 133
Climate Convention, 141
Cocoa and coffee, 15, 61, 63
Collor de Mello, Fernando, 19,
 107
Columbus, Christopher, 11
Cooperatives, 102, 110
Costa Marques, 61
Council of Bishops, 105
Crime, 56
Cuiabá, 1, 61
Cupuaçu, 102

Debt relief, 135
Deforestation, 58, 135
Democratic Rural Union (UDR),
 84, 85–86
Dragas, 46, 47, 49–50, 52, 53, 54,
 55, 57

Earth Summit conference, 33,
 133, 139–43
Economist magazine, 133
Education, 110
 forestry management, 31–32
 lack of schools, 40, 72
 literacy programs, 102
 malnutrition and, 37

El Dorado, 1, 3, 50
Electricity, 39, 40
Empates, 110
Employment, lack of, 37
Empty wilderness, myth of the,
 3
Extinction vs. integration, 2, 18
Extractive reserves, 75, 102, 115

Farming, 58–75, 134–35
 fish, 134
Fazenda Vista Alegre, 76–87
Federal Indian Authority
 (FUNAI), 11, 15, 17, 18, 52,
 107, 110, 136, 137
Fiscal incentives, 32–33, 76,
 80–81
Floodplains, 36, 134
Fofocas, 54
Food supplies, 2
 food on the floodplains, 134
 malnutrition, 37
Ford, Henry, 97
Forestry management, 24–33,
 135
 forest burning, 77
Friends of the Earth, 138
FUNTAC, 31

Garimpeiros, 52, 53, 54, 56, 57,
 107
Garimpos, 46, 49, 55, 74, 133, 137
Genipapo, 14
Goiás, 131
Gold mining, 3, 18, 36, 38,
 45–57
Great Snake, 41

Greenhouse effect, 77
Gross domestic product (GDP), 80
Guaraná, 63, 83, 102

Hardwood replanting program, 33
Health care, low level of, 133
  clinics, 17, 43
  drugs/drug companies, 2, 20
  herbal medicine, 40
  high pregnancy rates, 37
  malaria, 37, 40, 43, 56, 59, 62, 94
  malnutrition, 37
  pharmacy, 40
Horses, quarter, 83
Housing, 14, 17, 37, 130

Idealists, 104–16
Indian Statute, 12, 20
Indians, forest, 2, 8, 9–20, 61–62, 84, 95, 102
Indigenous Missionary Council, 105, 107
Insects, 3
International funding agencies, 137
International Tropical Timber Organization, 113

Jaguars, 41, 67

Land Settlement Board (INCRA), 111
Loggers, 21–33, 107
  logging and wood process-ing, 132
  selling timber to, 15, 18, 131

Madeira River, 60
Malaria, 37, 40, 43, 56, 59, 62, 94
Malocas, 14, 17, 130
Manioc, 37, 39, 40
Mapinguarí, 41
Marreteiros, 70–71
Mate, 70
Mato Grosso, 1
Mencragnotire Kayapó Indians, 19, 20
Mendes, Chico, 6, 79, 82, 84, 86, 88n, 100, 102, 103, 106, 128
Mercury, 18, 48–49, 53, 56
Migrants, rich, 7
Minas Gerais, 27–28, 59, 60
Mineral resources in Amazônia, 3, 19, 51–52
Miners, 45–57

National Council of Rubber Tappers, 100, 109
National Integration Program (1970), 59
'92 Global Forum (the People's Summit), 139, 140, 142–43
Non-governmental organizations (NGOS), 108–9, 140

Ouro Preto do Oeste, 61

Paiter, 16
Pajé, 16
Pará, 42, 60
Paraguay River, 2

Paraná, 60, 65, 66, 69
Pastoral Lands Commission, 105
Pasturelands, 63, 72, 77, 80, 81
Pedro Peixoto scheme, 65, 68, 69–70
Pimenta Buena, 117–19
Plácido de Castro, 88–103
Planafloro, 63, 74–75
Plywood, 30–31
Polonoroeste project, 3, 25–26, 59–63, 72–73
Poronga, 98
Porto Velho, 1, 39, 60, 72, 92, 119–22
"Profile of a River Community," 36
Pro-Indian Commission, 11, 105
Projeto Seringueiro, 110–11

Quinari, 64, 65

Ranchers, 76–87, 101, 135
Raoni, 12
Reforestation, 24–29, 132–33, 136
Reformed Lutheran Church, 65
Ribeirinhos, 60, 61
Rio Branco, 9, 11, 64, 66, 95, 101, 116, 122–25
Rio de Janeiro, 16, 84
   Earth Summit, 139–43
River people, 34–44, 133–34
Road to the Pacific, 7, 77, 78, 97
Roads, lack of paved, 7–8, 23, 37, 44, 62, 71

Rondônia, 1, 3–4, 5–8, 42, 59, 85
Rondônia Electric Company (CERON), 30
Rubber Army, 96–97, 98
Rubber tappers, 6, 20, 27, 68, 70, 78, 84, 88–103, 135–36

Santos, João Orestes Schneider dos, 50–51
São Paulo, 12, 56, 60, 84, 101
Seringal Triunfo, 88–103
Seringueiros, 96, 97, 100, 101, 102, 106, 109–10, 113, 114, 115, 136
Settlement schemes, 6, 10, 32, 43, 66–73
Settlers, 8, 58–75, 134–35
Soils, unsuitable, 6, 61, 62
State Environmental Institute, Acre, 111
Sting, 11, 12, 19
Suruí Indians, 15, 19, 22, 25
Survival International, 11
Sustainable development, 73–74

Television, 43
Third World Network, 141–42
Transamazônica, 59, 60
TransCoca Highway, 2, 124
Transport, poor, 6, 43, 62, 72
Tucuruí dam, 22

Union of Indigenous Nations (UNI), 11–12, 14, 131
United Nations Conference on

Environment and Development (UNCED), 139, 141
United Nations Environmental Program (UNEP), 141
Uru Eu Wau Wau Indians, 62
Usufruct, 78

Vargas, Getulio, 60, 76n
VARIG, 49
Várzeas, 36
Veja magazine, 51

White man's impact on Indians, 10–11, 20, 131
Wildlife Management Program, 113
Worker's Council of Amazônia, 109
World Bank, 26, 60
World War II, 96–97

Xapuri, 76–87, 125–29

Yanomami Indians, 19, 107, 108

Zoró, 17